Distinguished Studies in

American Legal and Constitutional History

Edited by
Harold Hyman
William P. Hobby
Professor of History
Rice University

A Garland Series

Distinguished Studies in American Legal and Constitutional History

1. Gary J. Aichele. *Legal Realism and Twentieth-Century American Jurisprudence: The Changing Consensus.*
2. Kenneth R. Bowling. *Politics in the First Congress, 1789–1791.*
3. Steven R. Boyd. *The Constitution in State Politics: From the Calling of the Constitutional Convention to the Calling of the First Federal Elections.*
4. Martin J. Costello. *Hating the Sin, Loving the Sinner: The Minneapolis Childrens' Theatre Company Adolescent Sexual Abuse Prosecutions.*
5. Richard S. Eckert. *The Gentlemen of the Profession: The Emergence of Lawyers in Massachusetts, 1630–1810.*
6. C. Ashley Ellefson. *The County Courts and the Provincial Court in Maryland, 1733–1763.*
7. James C. Foster. *The Ideology of Apolitical Politics: Elite Lawyers' Response to the Legitimation Crisis of Liberal-Capitalism, 1870–1920.*
8. Patrick M. Garry. *The American Vision of the Free Press: An Historical and Constitutional Revisionist View of the Press as a Marketplace of Ideas.*
9. Robert M. Goldman. *'A Free Ballot and a Fair Count': The Department of Justice and the Enforcement of Voting Rights in the South, 1877–1893.*
10. James W. Gordon. *Lawyers in Politics: Mid-Nineteenth Century Kentucky as a Case Study.*
11. Frederick K. Grittner. *White Slavery: Myth, Ideology, and American Law.*
12. Walter T. Hitchcock. *Timothy Walker: Antebellum Lawyer.*
13. Wythe Holt. *Virginia's Constitutional Convention of 1901–1902.*
14. John W. Johnson. *The Dimensions of Non-Legal Evidence in the American Judicial Process: The Supreme Court's Use of Extra-Legal Materials in the Twentieth Century.*
15. John M. Lindley. *'A Soldier is Also A Citizen': The Controversy over Military Justice in the U. S. Army, 1917–1920.*
16. Lester G. Lindley. *The Impact of the Telegraph on Contract Law.*
17. W. Ray Luce. Cohens v. Virginia *(1821), The Supreme Court and State Rights: A Reevaluation of Influences and Impacts.*
18. Stephen Middleton. *Ohio and the Antislavery Activities of Attorney Salmon Portland Chase, 1830–1849.*
19. Stephen M. Millett. *The Constitutionality of Executive Agreements: An Analysis of* United States v. Belmont.
20. Samuel N. Pincus. *The Virginia Supreme Court, Blacks, and the Law, 1870–1902.*
21. H. D. Rosenthal. *Their Day in Court: A History of the Indian Claims Commission.*
22. Peter E. Russell. *His Majesty's Judges: Provincial Society and the Supreme Court in Massachusetts, 1692–1774.*
23. Keith R. Schlesinger. *The Power that Governs: The Evolution of Judicial Activism in a Midwestern State, 1840–1890.*
24. Stephen K. Shaw. *The Ninth Amendment: Preservation of the Constitutional Mind.*
25. John M. Spivack. *Race, Civil Rights, and the United States Court of Appeals for the Fifth Judicial Circuit.*
26. Beverly Zweiben. *How Blackstone Lost the Colonies: English Law, Colonial Lawyers, and the American Revolution.*

How Blackstone Lost the Colonies

English Law, Colonial Lawyers, and the American Revolution

Beverly Zweiben

Garland Publishing, Inc.
New York & London
1990

Library of Congress Cataloging-in-Publication Data

Zweiben, Beverly.
How Blackstone lost the colonies : English law, colonial lawyers, and the American Revolution / Beverly Zweiben.
p. cm. — (Distinguished studies in American legal and constitutional history)
Includes bibliographical references.
ISBN 0-8240-0032-3
1. Law—United States—History and criticism. 2. United States—Constitutional history. I. Title. II. Series
KF352.Z74 1990
349.73—dc20
[347.3 90-32199

FOR MY MOTHER,

AND THE MEMORY OF MY FATHER,

AND FOR BILL

CONTENTS

AUTHOR'S PREFACE

In the almost two decades since I first approached the problem of defining the impact of English legal traditions on the American revolution, the academic community has been spurred in its thinking by two bicentennial celebrations, that of the Declaration of Independence and the United States Constitution. The result has been increased focus by scholars trained in both history and law on the strong commitment to legal precepts as the basis in eighteenth-century thought for English and colonial society. Indeed, there is general confirmation of my original thesis that "Blackstone lost the colonies" in codifying a theory of relationships that colonial lawyers could not ignore, and could not accept.

There are several scholars whose recent work highlights this trend toward greater appreciation of the relevance of law to our ongoing debate over the causes and meaning of the American Revolution. Jack Greene's recent review essay, "From the Perspective of Law: Context and Legitimacy in the Origins of the American Revolution," discusses the major contribution of legal historians to the neo-whig tradition. Greene points out that "colonial arguments on behalf of constitutional limits on metropolitan authority over the colonies, so long and so widely regarded as ad hoc, contrived, and insubstantial, now has to be regarded as having strong legal as well as experiential foundations."[1] Greene, and others, underscore the important contributions of John Phillip Reid to an understanding of law at center stage of the revolution.[2] An interesting review of Reid's work by Stephen Conrad focuses on the peculiar importance of legalism in American history, virtually from the outset. Conrad argues that the "epic pretense to legalistic justification made many differences in how the story of the ultimate alienation of the colonies unfolded...."[3]

The interested reader will find a useful analysis of the boundary between political and legal history in a series of essays on this subject collected by Hendrik Hartog, provocatively entitled <u>Law in the American Revolution and the Revolution in the Law</u>.[4] Also, Jack Greene and Bernard Bailyn have contributed to a collection of essays edited by Stephen Kurtz and James H. Hutson as the product of a bicentennial symposium at the Institute of Early American History and Culture in Williamsburg, Virginia. In

---

1 Greene, Jack P., "From the Perspective of Law: Context and Legitimacy in the Origins of the American Revolution," <u>South Atlantic Quarterly</u>. 1986 85(1): 56-77.

2 Reid, John Phillip, <u>Constitutional History of the American Revolution: The Authority of Rights,</u> (Madison, 1986).

3 Conrad, Stephen A., <u>William and Mary Quarterly</u>, 3d ser., 45(Oct 88), 775-778.

4 Hartog, Hendrik, ed., <u>Law in the American Revolution and the Revolution in American Law. A Collection of Review Essays in American Legal History.</u> New York University School of Law Series in Legal History:3. New York, 1981.

this interesting volume, Bailyn discusses the relationship of ideas as translated into resistance and revolution. Greene's essay is noteworthy for his analysis of the Bailyn, Caroline Robbins, J.G.A. Pocock theories of the imperial-colonial relationship.[5]

A longer work by Pocock, Politics, Language, and Time: Essays on Political Thought and History, delves into the transition from Coke to Blackstone and the role this transition played in shaping English history.[6]

Blackstone's influence on the American colonies is carefully evaluated by J. R. Pole, in his book Paths to the American Past, with particular reference to Blackstone's impact on James Wilson. This connection is also examined in an earlier volume, The Pursuit of Equality in American History.[7] Also, see an essay by Stanley Katz, "The Legal and Religious Context of Natural Rights Theory: A Comment," for a bibliographical essay on the treatment of legal aspects of political ideology. Katz underscores the use of legal arguments as an essential ingredient in political appeals for independence.[8]

---

5 Kurtz, Stephen G. and James H. Hutson, ed., Essays on the American Revolution. (Chapel Hill, 1973).

6 Pocock, J.G. A., Politics, Language, and Time: Essays on Political Thought and History. (New York, 1973.)

7 J.R. Pole, Paths to the American Past. (Oxford, 1979); and The Pursuit of Equality in American History. (Berkeley, 1978.)

8 Katz, Stanley N., "The Legal and Religious Context of Natural Rights Theory: A Comment," in Bonomi, Patricia, ed., Party and Political Opposition in Revolutionary

For a good general survey of the history of American law in its substance, procedure, and legal institutions, see the chapter on the colonial period in Lawrence Friedman's History of American Law. (New York, 1973.) Forrest McDonald offers to redress the balance of the "ideological school" in its disregard of the law and legal institutions, in his book Novus Ordo Seclorum: The Intellectual Origins of the Constitution. (Lawrence, 1985.)

For more specific application of the legal tradition to individual lawyers, see A.G. Roeber's Faithful Magistrates and Republican Lawyers: Creators of Virginia Legal Culture, 1680-1810. (Chapel Hill, 1981.) Also, Edward Dumbauld's Thomas Jefferson and the Law. (Norman, 1978.) for a detailed study of Jefferson's legal practice. John E. O'Connor's William Paterson, Lawyer and Statesman, 1745-1806 (Rutgers, 1979) examines the importance of law and its relationship to history as the underpinnings of Paterson's political ideology.

Readers interested in the path of the Enlightenment in Philadelphia, and elsewhere, will enjoy Henry F. May's The Enlightenment in America (Oxford, 1976). May offers a broad assessment of the impact of the enlightenment and argues that Philadelphia's politicians were mostly lawyers and mostly conservative. James Wilson, May concludes, was "the embodiment of Enlightenment and moderate conservatism."

America. (Tarrytown, 1980).

J.R. Pole describes Wilson's response to the "challenge of Parliament" as a rejection of Parliament's power in favor of the king's separate reign, essentially a crisis over the legitimacy of British institutions.[9] For a study of Wilson's application of his revolutionary experience to post-revolutionary nationalism, see George M. Dennison's "The Revolution Principle: Ideology and Constitutionalism in the Thought of James Wilson," Review of Politics (1977), 157-191. Morton G. White offers an interesting analysis of Wilson's philosophy of ethics and natural law in his volume on The Philosophy of the American Revolution. (Oxford, 1978).

Many traditional historians view Joseph Galloway as an appendage to Benjamin Franklin. Benjamin H. Newcomb documents the close relationship between Franklin and Galloway, and their eventual split.[10] Although Newcomb acknowledges Galloway's "legal mind," he ignores Galloway's legal training as a basis for his political perspectives. Instead, Newcomb points to "a field of vision too narrow to comprehend the American claims to freedom from parliamentary taxation." Newcomb added that "the lawyer was never quite certain what his position ought to be, and until 1776 he was reluctant to make a firm, final commitment."

---

9 Pole, J.R., The Gift of Government: Political Responsibility from the English Restoration to American Independence. (Athens, 1983).

10 Newcomb, Benjamin H., Franklin and Galloway: A Political Partnership. (New Haven, 1972).

John E. Ferling has attempted several studies of Galloway's ideology.[11] Although Ferling offers an insightful description of Galloway's thinking within the context of eighteenth-century philosophy, he neglects to tie Galloway's ideas to his legal background. Ferling argues that "Galloway's journey to exile, his failure, was partially of his own making. He consciously, rationally chose to remain loyal; he was privy to the same intellectual forces as the Whigs, and he might have chosen, as they did, to support the rebellion."

John Dickinson has benefitted from a recent biography by Milton E. Flower, published for the Friends of the John Dickinson Mansion.[12] Flower's biography fills the void left by earlier efforts by Charles J. Stille in 1891 and more recent articles by John H. Powell in that it provides a detailed description of Dickinson's legal training and offers important insight into colonial legal practice and the active role of lawyers in colonial society. For a popular analysis of the "Farmer's Letters", see M.E. Bradford's "A Better Guide Than Reason: The Politics of John Dickinson," Modern Age (1977), 39-49. Hopefully, Flower's

---

11 Ferling, John E., The Loyalist Mind: Joseph Galloway and the American Revolution. (Pa. State University Press, 1977); "Joseph Galloway: A Reassessment of the Motivations of a Pennsylvania Loyalist," Pennsylvania History, (April, 1972); "Compromise or Conflict: The Rejection of the Galloway Alternative to Rebellion," Pennsylvania History (1976), 5-22.

12 Flower, Milton E., John Dickinson, Conservative Revolutionary. (Charlottesville, 1983).

biography of Dickinson, and the work of historians attempting to understand the legal context of colonial America will refocus those who ascribe to the "Farmer's Letters" "obvious and perhaps deliberate misuse of facts and historical events...."[13] This same author endorses Sir Lewis Namier's view that contemporary discussions of the constitutional and political issues were simple and trite.

The work of the past two decades, of which this essay reflects only a part, offers encouragement that the lines dividing history and law will once again be joined, as they were, indeed, in the eighteenth century.

---

[13] Chaffin, Robert J., "Whig vs. Tory: The Ideological Response to the Townshend Acts of 1767," North Dakota Quarterly (1977), 5-18.

CHAPTER ONE

INTRODUCTION

A dozen years after Great Britain won the war for empire in North America her thirteen colonies proposed to undo the results of that feat by declaring independence. A year earlier, Edmund Burke had made a number of important, yet unheeded, observations on the Anglo-colonial situation. In his speech to Parliament "On Conciliation with the Colonies," Burke pointed to the "mutuality of tradition, the shared temper and character" which dominated the Atlantic civilization. The English, he warned, could not longer isolate the large and growing colonial population outside the protective shield of the English constitution, or restrict them to a "partial, narrow, contracted, pinched, occasional system...."[1] Burke emphasized the shared "love of Freedom" which motivated both branches of Englishmen. Far-off descendants of Englishmen in the colonies maintained their ardor and devotion to law and liberty to a degree forgotten by eighteenth-century Englishmen at home.[2] The key to the colonial position was the law and the large numbers of American lawyers. Burke said:

> In no country perhaps in the world is the law so general a study. The profession itself is numerous and powerful, and in most provinces it takes the lead. The greater number of deputies sent to the congress were lawyers. But all who read,

> and most do read, endeavor to obtain some smattering of that science....This study renders men acute, inquisitive, dexterous. prompt in attack, ready in defence, and full of resources....They anticipate the evil, and judge of the pressure of the grievances by the badness of the principle. They augur misgovernment at a distance and sniff the approach of tyranny in every tainted breeze.[3]

Burke added another piece of pertinent information: the colonists were buying law books in numbers second only to traditionally popular religious books. And they were buying Blackstone's Commentaries with enthusiasm barely exceeded in the home market.

Burke perceived that the interest in law volumes and in Blackstone revealed concern for America's relationship to the underlying English institutions of statutes, custom, and common law. Because all Englishmen paid these at least verbal homage, Burke added that an Englishman is the unfittest person on earth to argue another Englishman into slavery."[4] For the same reason an Englishman was unlikely to submit to new British policy. The salient point here is that Burke assumed a close relationship between English law, colonial lawyers, and the American revolution.

It is my thesis that the colonists perceived their revolution as a crisis within the English legal system -- a constitutional framework in which they shared the rights and obligations of all Englishmen. The decisions reached by 1776, whether for loyalism or for patriotism, were grounded in respect for legal processes, reverence for the didactic authority of the past, and a commitment to the relevance of the past to the present. Colonial lawyers, trained in English law, yet rooted in the American environment, found themselves the middlemen between the old tradition and the new circumstance.

When James Wilson gave the new nation its first series of law lectures at the University of Pennsylvania in 1790, his theme was the development of a legal code and philosophy which reflected the American experience: not surprisingly, he attacked the legal philosophy of Sir William Blackstone. Wilson and Blackstone (the latter had inaugurated law lectures at Oxford University in 1753) shared, however, a common perception of the law's development. They agreed that, as Wilson put it, "Law should be studied and taught as a historical science."[5] Blackstone was more explicit on this point. He wrote in the _Commentaries_ that the law's basic principles

> should be traced to their fountains...; to the customes of the Britons and Germans, as recorded by Caesar and Tacitus: to the codes of the Northern nations on the Continent, and more especially to those of our Saxon princes; to the Rules of the Roman law...but above all, to the inexhaustible reservoir of legal antiquities and learning, to the feudal law, or...the law of nations in our western orb.[6]

Blackstone's reliance on the past as a source of wisdom was not unique to lawyers. Englishmen in the seventeenth and eighteenth centuries had looked upon the past not only as a record of previous events, but as a "lamp of experience" which led enlightened men through the labyrinth of their own day. History provided cumulative wisdom, a touchstone which guided men away from previous political errors and taught them to cherish traditions proved true and noble by time and earlier generations.[7]

English common law gained its authority because it, too, had stood the test of cumulative wisdom and continuous adaptability.[8] That standard became the measure of English institutions; Englishmen called upon the past to support the law's antiquity and the continuity of England's political and legal heritage.

The colonial problem, of course, was the transfer of a sophisticated and complex legal system to a more simple society. For colonists studying English law the historical perspective cleared the way for two responses: first, Americans maintained a sense of legal continuity between themselves and the principles of the ancient constitution; second, the concept of the common law as continuously adaptable permitted colonists to justify the local modification of procedure, without necessarily diminishing the principles of the English tradition.

The basic premise of the ancient constitution was that fundamental law had ruled since the mythic origins of the English people, although the law's original perfection had tarnished with time. The ancient precepts had dictated balanced power between ruler and ruled: the king was subject to the law and the people spoke their will through their representatives. Seventeenth and eighteenth century political activists relied on this principle as a means of communication between Englishmen of different political persuasions: reforms were necessary to return the ancient constitution to its old luster.[9]

For their view of antiquity English whigs turned to Tacitus, particularly to Germania, which described the egalitarian mores of that primitive people who became England's forbears. As we shall see, seventeenth-century supporters of Parliament extrapolated from the Germans' primitive procedures around the campfire a code of conduct which reinforced concepts of limited monarchy and balanced Government of an ancient vintage.[10]

Showing continuity in the English experience proved much more troublesome, primarily because of William of Normandy; 1066 caused the whigs great trauma. They had wed themselves to an equation of past to present, that is, any prerogative claimed and implemented by a king or assembly in the eleventh century continued undiminished down to the seventeenth century. Therefore, because Parliament claimed that the Stuarts were subject to the rule of law, they must prove equal subordination for William. Further, they felt obliged to defend William's claim to the throne on hereditary grounds. If William the Norman were, indeed, William the Conqueror, then England's political continuity had been broken and the rule of law fallen before the king's sword. In this same tenor, whigs (Coke here is exemplary) ignored the introduction of feudalism which, of course, implied homage and obligations of the tenants-in-chief to the king and, therefore, the subordination of the national assembly. The whigs were forced to assert that

William had legal rights to the throne of England and within that legality he had accepted a pre-existing body of laws to which he was subordinate. These principles, with minor changes to rectify the moral lapse from the ancient constitution, were reaffirmed in the thirteenth century and after in the form of Magna Carta.

The moral of the tale became clear. The whig interpretation reached its peak during the seventeenth century, when parliamentary power raised its head at the cost of royal prerogative. The common law, whigs claimed, restricted the king's power and status. They pointed to the ancient Germans. Tacitus described the royal figure as merely a peer among peers, a man originally chosen for primacy as a skilled military leader. His was not an hereditary office, but one which had evolved through merit of person. Further evidence of kingly subordination centered around William's political legitimacy and the more than thirty confirmations of Magna Carta after 1215.

As the whigs subordinated royal prerogative, they also raised the power of Parliament. Parliament, they claimed, represented a popular voice which had functioned prior to and coexistent with the monarchy. German tribesmen around the campfire, making decisions by voice vote, including the choice of their leader, provided the first evidence of a parliament's existence. And in the seventeenth century, the whigs dusted off Magna Carta to claim that the freemen of 1215 lived on as the commons of 1628 and 1688.

Parliament's victory in 1641 had made Coke its spokesmen and the arbiter of English common law. His theme was the common law authority for limiting extensive royal prerogative in favor of Parliament's rightful authority. The great emphasis on Magna Carta grew out of Coke's assertion that it encompassed all that was fundamental in English law. Coke wrote, "It was for the most part declaratory of the principal grounds of the fundamental laws of England, and for the residue it is additional to supply some defects of the common law; and it was no new declaration...."[11] As fundamental law it became Coke's criteria for constitutionally: "if any judgment be given contrary to any of the points of the great charter,...by the justices, or by any other kings, ministers, etc. it shall be undone, and holden for naught."[12]

Coke's interpretation of Magna Carta limited the king's power to tax by demanding parliamentary consent for all extraordinary grants to the crown. Without that safeguard, token revenues might grow from precedent to tradition to economic slavery. Especially dangerous were taxes granted in the press of war which tended to continue into peacetime. Coke observed that "when any ancient law or custome of parliament is broken, and the Crown possessed of a precedent, how difficult a thing it is to restore the subject again to his former freedoms and safety."[13] Magna Carta, he claimed, protected against taxation without the "grant and common assent in parliament."[14]

The "common law mind" pervaded both whig and Tory camps. Tories, too, bowed to the tyranny of antiquity and sought to prove that the ancient constitution subordinated law and Parliament to royal prerogative. They claimed, of course, what William had conquered England, that in doing so he had confiscated all English lands and distributed the property to his followers in exchange for feudal homage. This was the key. William had introduced feudal tenure and the Norman legal system. By the royal writ laws were made. By the royal writ nobles were called to pay homage to their king, not as his equal, but as his subordinate. Magna Carta, they claimed, may have redefined this relationship, but these were innovations won by force and they applied only too the nobility. The conclusion? Royal supremacy -- to law, to Parliament -- molded the English constitution, a supremacy for which the tories also looked backward to the ancient constitution.

Of course, Coke had applied the teachings of antiquity and the common law to restrict royal prerogative and to shore up Parliament's role as defender of England's ancient constitution. The colonists who read Coke were not so specific. The Institutes became a morality play wherein extensive prerogative, in whatever guise, was held at bay by common law in the name of property rights and representative government. In the eighteenth century the spirit of Magna Carta seemed to authorize resistance to discriminatory taxation by Parliament in much the way Kings John, Henry III, Charles I, and James II, had been resisted, also in the name of property rights and representative government. Perhaps Coke was nowhere more relevant to colonial lawyers than when he advised Parliament: "A good caveat to parliaments is to leave all causes to be measured by the golden and streight metewand of the law, and not by the uncertain and crooked cord of discretion....It is not almost incredible to foresee, when any maxim or fundamental law of this realm is altered (as elsewhere hath been observed) what dangerous inconveniences doe follow..."[15]

The structures of the common law tradition in which all lawyers were trained had twofold implications: first, it reinforced the identification between representation and the rule of law; second, it provided precedent with which to rectify political imbalance through the monarch -- limited by contractual relationships and himself subordinate to the law.

The common law tradition was reinforced from innumerable sources, perhaps explaining why so many lawyers accepted its principles. Thomas Jefferson's Commonplace Book, for example, in which he recorded his reading in the law, revealed the wide variety of legal materials which emphasized royal subordination to the law and the legal guarantees traditionally accorded Englishmen.[16]

Many of the standard texts Jefferson read on feudal tenure or property rights underscored the voluntary or legal transition to feudal tenure, or the simultaneous existence of totally private ownership of land. For example, Robertson.s History of Charles V, a history of feudal property, indicated that in the Roman empire (with which the British identified) the nature of property rights was ambiguous. No feudal tenure was involved, however, because, as Robertson wrote, military service was voluntary "from attachment, not from a sense of obligation." Tacitus, the traditional authority on Rome and the German tribes, supported the theory of the voluntary origins of feudal relationships: "Allodial property," he wrote, "was frequently converted into feudal, by a voluntary deed of the possessor." He argued that feudal relationships had stemmed from the need for a powerful protector from anarchy. Francis Stoughton Sullivan, in his _An Historical Treatise on the Feudal Laws and the Constitution and Laws of England_, written in 1772, added that although the king had full power to distribute lands, his power was limited by a "prudent discretion" in order to prevent rebellion. When conflicting interpretations occurred, Jefferson sided with whigs and liberty.

Sir John Dalrymple and William Somner disagreed on the extent of feudal tenure. Dalrymple wrote in 1757 that all English lands were held in feudal tenure after William the Conqueror; Somner had written that there were many examples of land held after the conquest without obligation. Jefferson, noting the conflict between the two, concluded that "surely he (Somner) was the better Saxon scholar."[17] Blackstone, of course, capped the whig perspective. Of William and the introduction of feudalism, he wrote, "This new polity therefore seems not to have been imposed by the conqueror but adopted by the general assembly of the whole realm....English liberties are...a restoration of that antient constitution of which our ancestors had been defrauded by the art and finesse of the Norman lawyers, rather than deprived by the force of Norman arms."[18]

Jefferson's sources, and Jefferson himself, accepted the implicit significance of William's introduction of feudalism and the implications of that institution for seventeenth and eighteenth-century society; feudalism by the king's authority jeopardized the rule of law and the legal independence of Englishmen and Americans. Jefferson, in his Summary View, felt called upon to insist that feudalism did not exist prior to William; further, William had distributed only those lands which belonged to men killed at the Battle of Hastings, leaving the land of other Saxons in private ownership. He wrote: "Our Saxon ancestors held their lands, as they did their personal property, in absolute dominion, disencumbered with any superior...." Although some land became subject to feudal distribution,:

> much was left in the hands of his (William's) Saxon subjects, held of no superior, and not subject to feudal considerations. But still they had not been surrendered to the King, they were not derived from his grant, and therefore they were not holden of him....Feudal holdings were therefore but exceptions out of Saxon laws of possession, under which all lands were held in absolute right. These therefore still form the basis or groundwork of the Common law....America was not conquered by William the Norman, nor its lands surrendered to him or any of his successors.[19]

Blackstone's Commentaries clearly posed the dilemma they tried to resolve: the Glorious Revolution had guaranteed to Englishmen security of property and person through parliamentary omnipotence. The settlement, which resolved the centuries-old problem of royal prerogative, did not, however, prescribe for the empire which was only then taking shape. When Blackstone attempted to resolve that constitutional law, he reached conclusions which Americans, versed in English law, believed deprived them of their rights. Although Blackstone bolstered their view of the timeless and irrevocable nature of English legal guarantees, he excluded the colonists from their provisions. Further, he underscored Parliament's omnipotence in North America.

After 1763 Americans began to consider themselves vulnerable to a tyranny by Parliament equivalent to the royal Stuart tyranny against which Englishmen had twice revolted during the previous century. John Adams, in 1789, compared the British constitution to a "three legged stool." "If one leg is longer than another," Adams wrote, "The stool will not stand."[20] The royal leg, to use Adams' analogy, had been shortened by Parliament in the seventeenth century; in the eighteenth century Americans tendered Parliament a similar service.

On this point a loyalist, Joseph Galloway, agreed with patriots such as John Dickinson and James Wilson: parliamentary omnipotence violated the spirit of English freedoms and the intent of the Glorious Revolution. Galloway ultimately parted from Dickinson and Wilson in his perception of the growth of the English constitution and the role of English colonies within the imperial structure. But in the years 1763 to 1776, colonial lawyers struggled in common with these problems: what were the boundaries of the English constitution in the eighteenth century? How could Americans resolve the ambiguities within the constitutional structure and yet retain the legal rights they believed were guaranteed to all Englishmen?

Blackstone had written, and the colonists agreed, that parliamentary supremacy was the result of the Glorious Revolution and represented a concept of "body politic" characteristic of the new nationalism. It was a logical step, then, for colonial lawyers to respond to what they considered parliamentary oppression by denying that the Glorious Revolution had completed Britain's search for constitutional government.

The British constitution was ambiguous on a number of points: the ill-defined political jurisdiction of the colonies was only one example. Another problem was that the legal structure retained many elements of feudalism, especially on the question of land tenure. It was still a principle in the law, for example, that all land originated with the king; further, land tenure remained the only basis for political participation.[21] When Wilson and Dickinson searched, in the fashion of lawyers, for precedents within the English legal system with which to circumvent Parliament's omnipotence they turned to these remnants of England's feudal tradition.

The search for an imperial framework which would guarantee rights of Englishmen for Americans and adequately define colonial political jurisdiction took place in three stages between 1763 and 1776. Initially (1763 to 1768) colonial theories of empire were vague. Dickinson, for example, made fuzzy distinctions between taxation and regulation of trade, while admitting that Parliament retained the right to legislature. The second (and pivotal) stage (1770 to 1775) saw the reemergence of the feudal strain. Unlike the first stage, the second permitted the colonists to develop a coherent, although short-lived theory of imperial structure which guaranteed to their assemblies the legislative rights inherent in the English doctrine of representative government. Equally important, the colonies held on to membership in the empire at the same time that they denied to Parliament legislative authority in America.

Essentially, colonial lawyers claimed that their English nationality stemmed from their ties to the king of England. The important point was that they rejected loyalty to the "body politic" in favor of the feudal concept of allegiance to the person of the king from whom, they argued, had come the original land grants. The king did not have the right to legislate for them--they had assemblies for that purpose -- but the tie between king and subject transcended geography. They found precedents for this relationship in the whig views of Coke's Institutes and in the decision in Calvin's Case or Postnati (1608) which, to put it briefly, permitted Scotsmen born after 1603 to share English naturalization through their relationship with James, although Scotland maintained its own legislature and legal code. This second state was crucial to the development of a revolutionary philosophy. The colonists had rejected as illegal Parliament's claim to legislative authority over the colonies: the only tie to the empire, they claimed, was through loyalty to the person of the king who provided them, in turn, with protection according to feudal theory. When, in 1775, George III lost that special distinction, the colonists had no alternative to parliamentary authority but independence. This was the third stage.

It must be pointed out at this juncture that colonial lawyers who accepted elements of the feudal tradition could not have done so had there not existed certain concepts which were deeply rooted in the "common law mind." The common law tradition perpetuated by Coke and other whigs conjured up a monarch subservient to the law and limited in his prerogatives by a contractual relationship between king and subjects. It was not to an absolute lord to whom the colonial lawyers turned but to the whig Monarch delineated in the basic text of English lawyers, Coke's. Institutes of the Laws of England.[22]

The feudal construct also created a wide gulf between patriot lawyers and those, like Galloway, who had totally rejected the concept of a personal monarch in the eighteenth century. Galloway envisioned the Glorious Revolution as the constitutional solution to the conflicts of centuries -- essentially the problem of royal prerogative. The battles of 1688 had secured for all Englishmen the right of political representation as a preservation of property rights. Parliament's claims after the French and Indian War violated those guarantees; the political structure of the empire must be revised, he decided, to protect American rights. To that end he proposed his Plan of Union. Parliament, under that Plan, could never again exercise unilateral sovereignty over Americans, as it could still do in Ireland. Galloway, who had never questioned the concept of parliamentary authority over the colonies, did repudiate Parliament's claim to unilateral political control over the colonies which denied colonists representation. In the end Galloway remained loyal to the idea of the body politic secured by the Glorious Revolution and chose allegiance to its personification, King, Lords, and Commons in Parliament, which he had hoped to reform, but could not reject.

The careers of Joseph Galloway, John Dickinson, and James Wilson, demand attention for a number of reasons: first, their writings highlight the importance of Anglo-Saxon legal traditions for the development of prerevolutionary political philosophy; second, they played central political roles in the colony which hosted the first and second Continental Congress and the Constitutional Convention; third, Pennsylvania's charter crisis of 1764 involved Galloway and Dickinson in a constitutional debate which foreshadowed the conflicts within the empire from the Stamp

Act to the Intolerable Acts; and fourth, the reputations and prestige of these men transcended the boundaries of their own colony and influenced the perceptions of all colonists aroused by the constitutional crises facing the British empire.

Dickinson has a unique reputation for being both "the penman of the Revolution" and "a great fortune and piddling genius."[23] The first half stemmed from his great fame in the early years (1765 to 1770) for important political statements which rejected on constitutional grounds Parliament's right to tax the colonists. He authored the resolutions of the Pennsylvania Assembly and of the Stamp Act Congress in opposition to the stamp tax. His literary monument' however, was his "Letters from a Farmer in Pennsylvania," written in 1768 against the Townshend program. In the "Farmer's Letters" Dickinson presented a coherent constitutional philosophy of American rights based on the English doctrine of representative government which remained the colonists' underlying theme. By 1774 Dickinson abandoned his earlier distinctions between taxation and the regulation of trade and committed himself to total rejection of Parliament's right to tax the colonies in any instance. Despite that strong position in his _Essay on the Constitutional Power of Great Britain over the Colonies_. Dickinson's reputation is shadowed by John Adams' damning phrase and his seeming conservatism at the crucial point in the revolution.

Adams' complaint was directed against the Olive Branch Petition to the King," 1775. But Dickinson committed a greater historical sin of omission -- he did not sign the Declaration of Independence for fear that the colonists were not sufficiently united to withstand the military power of the British army. In later days the omission plagued his reputation, despite his military role in the army, his contributions to the framing of the Articles of Confederation, the Constitutional Convention, and to Pennsylvania and Delaware as chief executive.[24]

James Wilson came late to the colonial scene -- not until 1765 did he arrive in New York from Scotland. In 1774, Wilson published a pamphlet he had written six years earlier, Considerations on the Nature and Extent of the Legislative Authority of the British Parliament. Wilson presented a coherent constitutional argument for rejecting all of Parliament's claims to legislative authority over the colonies. America's membership in the empire, he concluded, was based only on allegiance to the person of the king and the royal protection. Considerations conveys the full impact of Calvin's Case and the feudal tradition of seventeenth-century whigs.

Historians have treated these men to a kind of retroactive judgment based on the outcome of the Revolution: the triumph of nationalism and democracy in the nineteenth century. As a result, Galloway has been dismissed as a "loyalist" with all the disdain befitting a loser. Dickinson, too, fell partially into this category. He had doubted American military prowess against the British empire; therefore, he was a "conservative" guilty of faulty patriotism and vision. Wilson's reputation, to the contrary, has been glorified. In the Constitutional Convention of 1787, and in his law lectures in 1791, Wilson spoke of nationalism and popular sovereignty, both later glorified in American mythology.[25]

Two things are necessary to correct these images, first, these men must be seen within the context of their own day: second, they need to be recognized as lawyers devoted to the Anglo-Saxon legal tradition and trained in its perspectives, procedures, and myths. I hope to shed some light on the impact of English law on the American Revolution and on the role of American lawyers in developing a coherent constitutional theory of empire which brought the colonists to independence.

Footnotes

[1] Edmund Burke, Speech Moving Resolutions for Conciliation with the Colonies, March 22, 1775," *Works* (Boston, 1839), I, 24.

[2] *Ibid*.

[3] *Ibid*., 36-37.

[4] *Ibid*., 43.

[5] James Wilson, "Study of the Law," in Robert Green McCloskey, ed., *The Works of James Wilson* (Cambridge, 1967), I, 70.

[6] Sir William Blackstone, *Commentaries on the Laws of England* (New York, 1856), I, 34.

7 See H. Trevor Colbourn. *The Lamp of Experience, Whig History and the Intellectual Origins of the American Revolution* (Chapel Hill, 1965), 3-58; Bernard Bailyn, *The Ideological Origins of the American Revolution* (Cambridge, 1967), 22-54. Caroline Robbins, *The Eighteenth Century Commonwealthman, Studies in the Transmission. Development and Circumstance of English Liberal Thought from the Restoration of Charles II until the War with the Thirteen Colonies* (Cambridge, 1961); Thomas Jefferson to Col. Duane, April 4, 1813, in E. Millicent Sowerby, *Catalogue of the Library of Thomas Jefferson* (Library of Congress, 1952), I,1. Jefferson wrote: "I take refuge in the histories of other times, where if they also furnished their Catalines & Caligulas, their stories are handed to us under the brand of a Livy, a Sallust and a Tacitus, and we are comforted with the reflection that the condemnation of all

succeeding generations has confirmed the censures of the historian, and consigned their memories to everlasting infamy."

[8] Sir Matthew Hale, "Preface," to Henry Rolle, *Un Abridgement des Plusiers Cases et Resolutions del Common Ley* (London, 1668), 30. Hale wrote that the English common law was the product of much wisdom, Time and Experience."

[9] See J.G.A. Pocock, *The Ancient Constitution and the Feudal Law*, *A Study of English Historical Thought in the Seventeenth Century* (Cambridge, 1957), 182-228.

[10] Samuel Kliger, *The Goths in England*, *A Study in Seventeenth and Eighteenth Century Thought* (Cambridge, 1952), 1-111.

[11] Edward Coke, *Institutes of the Laws of England* (London, 1743), II, Preface.

[12] *Ibid*.

[13] *Ibid*., 528-29.

[14] *Ibid*., 533.

[15] *Ibid*., IV, 41.

[16] See Gilbert Chinard, ed., *The Commonplace Book of Thomas Jefferson*, *A Repertory of His Ideas on Government* (Baltimore, 1926). Jefferson used his commonplace book as a means or synthesizing each case according to its basic legal principles. He wrote of commonplacing: "it obliges the student to seek out the pith of the case, and habituates him to a condensation of thought....It fixes the case, too, more indelibly in the mind."

Quoted in Dumas Malone, Jefferson the Virginian (Boston, 1948), 72-73.

[17] Sir John Dalrymple, Essay Towards A General History of Feudal Property in Great Britain (London, 1957) William Somner, A Treatise of Gavelkind (London, 1660): See Jefferson, Commonplace Book, 189-90.

[18] Ibid., 136, 189-93, 229-31, 238-39.

[19] Thomas Jefferson, Summary View of the Rights of British America," On Julian Boyd, ed., The Papers of Thomas Jefferson (Princeton, 1950), I, 132-33.

[20] L. H. Butterfield, ed., Diary and Autobiography of John Adams (New York, 1964), III, 219 (hereafter cited as Diary).

[21] See Frederick W. Maitland, The Constitutional History of England (Cambridge, 1955), 141-164, 526-539.

[22] See Pocock. The Ancient Constitution, 30-56.

[23] Moses Coit Tyler, Literary History of the American Revolution (New York, 1897), II, 24, Adams, Diary, II, 162.

[24] John Dickinson, "To my Opponents in the Late Elections of Councillor for the County of Philadelphia, and of President of the Supreme Executive Council of Pennsylvania, 1783," Library of Congress, Manuscript Division. Dickinson had to answer charges that he had opposed the Declaration of Independence and disapproved of the Pennsylvania Constitution of 1776. For further biographical information, see Charles Stille, Life and Times of John Dickinson, 1732-1802 (Philadelphia, 1819); John H. Powell, "John Dickinson,

Penman of the American Revolution" (unpubl. Ph.D. diss., University of Iowa, 1938).

For Galloway, see Ernest H. Baldwin, Joseph Galloway: The Loyalist Politician (Philadelphia, 1902): Julian Boyd, Anglo-American Union, Joseph Galloway's Plan to Preserve the British Empire. 1774-1788 (Philadelphia, 1941): David L. Jacobson, John Dickinson and Joseph Galloway, 1764-1776, A Study in Contrasts" (unpubl. Ph.D. diss., Princeton University, 1959): Raymond Clarence Werner, "Joseph Galloway, His Life and Times" (unpubl. Ph.D. diss., University of Iowa, 1927).

[25] See Vernon L. Parrington, The Colonial Mind. 1620-1800 (New York. 1927), 224-237; Clinton Rossiter, The Political Thought of the American Revolution (New York, 1963), 67: McCloskey, ed., James Wilson. I, 80-81: Charles Page Smith, James Wilson: Founding Father, 1742-1798 (Chapel Hill, 1956), 230-246.

CHAPTER TWO

ENGLISH LAW AND COLONIAL LAWYERS

Historians have shown concern over the degree of professional training among colonial lawyers. One view is that colonial lawyers were merely "smatterers and admirers of the law" whose simple outlook liberated "American law from many of the shackles of English medievalism."[1]

This view is challenged by those who claim that although colonial law did not reproduce the full complexity found in England, neither did the colonists attempt to reproduce English society. To the extent that local circumstance and English regulations permitted, colonial law was remarkably sophisticated. Examples of colonial grasp of legal intricacies can be found in the Massachusetts Code of 1648. The Code was a comprehensive legal document dealing with crimes, torts, property rights, and domestic relations. Essentially, it provided a simplified version of English law: softer criminal penalties and debtor treatment, simpler rules of process; and it abolished primogeniture. Furthermore, Nathaniel Ward, who helped draft the Code, studied law before joining the ministry. The use of justices of the peace and technical forms of procedure (summons, writs of attachment and distraint, appeals, juries, and standard legal terms) support the assertion that the early legal system in Massachusetts revealed a remarkable degree of complexity.[2]

The issue of professionalism among colonial lawyers is obviously intertwined with the problem of transmission of English common law in America, that is, the greater the degree of sophistication and professionalism among colonial lawyers, the easier the transferal of common law concepts.

The rigor of training and the extent to which common law procedures were accepted varied from colony to colony. While the variance prevented inter-colonial uniformity of standards and procedure, there were also many benefits from that flexibility. In each colony criteria for legal training and admission to the bar was locally determined, which helped to create lawyers attuned to the social structure and intellectual perspectives of the people they represented. In many cases colonial lawyers participated in the economic and political life to their colony as merchants and landowners or as members of the assembly. As a result, colonial lawyers held pivotal positions in America based on their overlapping, mutually reinforcing roles as landed or mercantile interests, locally sustained political powers, and as arbiters of the legal criteria regulating all three.[3]

The influential role played by colonial lawyers in the coming of the Revolution stemmed from two sources. First, they were trained in English legal procedures and in the acknowledged principles of the common law mind. When English policy after 1763 created constitutional crises colonial lawyers were prepared to speak out for America's interpretation of English rights. This chapter will show that legal training in the colonies prepared its lawyers in the traditions of the common law mind and in the law's defense against unreasonable prerogative. Second, political roles in the assembly, and social and economic prestige provided colonial lawyers with the forums from which their voices were heard throughout colonial America. Sometimes the prestige was consciously created; the attempts at self-regulation described in this chapter is an example. For other lawyers, legal practice also provided avenues to political power or landed wealth, which made them pivotal members of society. Training and position combined to create in the legal profession middlemen for the ancient constitution in a new frontier.

John Adams complained during the early years of his law training that "A lawyer in this Country must study common Law, and Admiralty Law, and must do the duty of a Counsellor. a Lawyer, an Attorney, a solicitor, and even of a scrivener, so that the Difficulties of the Profession are much greater here than in England."[4] Perhaps it was English specialization, as well as the expense of London, which limited the number of colonials who took their training at the Inns of Court.

From 1750 to the American Revolution, over one hundred colonists undertook the pilgrimage to the Inns of Court, especially to Inner and Middle Temples. Many came from the South, especially South Carolina. Pennsylvania produced the second largest contingent, presumably because their English-based proprietor might act as spokesman and liaison. The American roster reads like a directory of prestigious colonial families. Among them were the Dulanys. father and son, Charles Carroll, Benjamin Chew, Thomas McKean, Edward Shippen, George Read, John Dickinson, and Jared Ingersoll.[5]

What went on in England was important for its being English. As a result many came to read English books in Middle Temple and hear cases in Westminster, rather than do these things in Philadelphia, or New York, or Charleston. They stayed for.prestige, occasionally better training, and the sometimes heady experience of proximity to a world of which they had only read. Benjamin Chew, for one, had complained to his father in 1743 from Middle Temple of the palling inactivity at Westminster' "there is so little business depending there that the Judges themselves agree it is hardly worth a students attendance."[6] But thirty years later, he advised his recalcitrant future son-in-law, Edward Tilghman, Jr., to remain in London. He wrote the boy that although the books were identical and office practice in the colonies had unique merits, nothing aided a lawyer's reputation as much as having been in Westminster.[7]

John Dickinson, on the contrary, wrote enthusiastically about his London experience. Dickinson had been born in 1732 in Maryland to a landed family which moved within a decade to Kent County, Delaware. He was the son of Samuel Dickinson, president and Judge of the Delaware Court of Common Pleas and, from 1754 to his death, associate judge of the Supreme Court. Dickinson studied first in the Office of John Moland, an influential Pennsylvania lawyer and then, in 1754, in the pattern of father and mentor, he went to study at the Inns of Court.

Dickinson was excited about the "living" quality of English law in practice and the practicing luminaries. And quite naturally, he was intrigued by the liberation provided by a sophisticated environment in which great political names manipulated English public life. In a first burst of enthusiasm Dickinson was captured by the romantic excitement of his environment. He could "hear" the ghosts of great legal names, Coke, Plowden, Hampden, and Holt, and longed to add "Dickinson."[8] He heard cases appealed before the King's Privy Council by eloquent spokesmen whose style he deemed incomparable.[9] As Dickinson absorbed the spirit of English courts, where "the very appearance of justice is awful, and the dress of the judges is calculated to inspire respect," he noted the "grandeur & solemnity of the courts of law" and lauded "their wisdom & knowledge."[10]

Dickinson soon began to have some reservations. He wrote home soon after his arrival of the "free will" among law students and its wide range of possibilities. He told his father, "Every person lives without controls in his chambers, & according to his disposition may either prosecute his studies with the greatest quiet in them, or employ them to the worst purpose."[11]

Dickinson gradually learned about English law. He considered the experience invaluable. He saw the learned and the ignorant, he read law, then heard it argued and analyzed in Westminster. He assured his father that "here we are not always plodding over books: Westminster Hall is a school of law where we not only hear what we have read repeated, but disputed in the most curious and learned manner, nay frequently hear things quite new, have our doubts cleared up, & our errors corrected. The barr is a perfect comment upon the written law, & every great man at it is in some measure a master & instructor to these young students who have the wisdom to attend here."[12] He continued to maintain that he who would look for professional advantage would find many opportunities for practical application, to meet successful practitioners, and what was perhaps best, to be challenged by other students who struggled with similar problems.[13]

The divergent experiences of John Dickinson, Benjamin Chew and Charles Carroll, testify that the Inns of Court did not themselves provide legal education. But legal education was available to those who attended the Inns. Members who dogged court sessions at Westminster, read and digested cases in commonplace books, then collated their readings with practical exercises could emerge trained to deal with basic and intricate problems of common law. Observers could well be critical of fluctuating criteria and pseudo-professional pretenses of the Inns of Court. But these were functional for a social scheme which coped with younger sons of a landed, primogeniture-laden society. At the Inns they might mark time, gain graces, and learn something of contractual pitfalls, all in an acceptable manner. These nuances of overindulgence merely reflected an age of many indulgences. Coke had written in the Institutes that whatever the peculiar qualities of common law, they were English peculiarities.[14] One might say the same of English lawyers.

The processes of gaining legal competence in the colonies were never stylized in the English fashion. The haphazard quality.of colonial.legal education prior to the Revolution stemmed from sketchy controls on procedure. A non-apprenticed student might stay home with reading list and texts and adapt himself to common-placing. Jefferson spent six years in such intermittent reading. Patrick Henry, his sometimes competitor, studied for six weeks (with differing results). Generally, the success of private reading depended on intelligent advice and the diligence and perception of the reader.

More commonly, a student paid an attorney for a seat in his office and instruction which varied from close supervision to education by osmosis. Some lawyers consistently produced better results than others. James Wilson studied with John Dickinson. Jeremiah Gridley influenced James Otis, Oxenbridge Thacher, Benjamin Prat, later chief justice of New York, and John Adams.

Otis studied with Gridley for seven years. His career, though short and quixotic, managed to earn the respect of his political enemy, Thomas Hutchinson.[15]

Joseph Galloway, like Dickinson, was born in 1732 into a family whose landed wealth had originated in Maryland. He moved to Philadelphia after his father's death, studied law locally, and, at the age of eighteen, he was admitted to practice before the Pennsylvania supreme court. Although the precise nature of Galloway's training is unknown, contemporaries have testified to the end result. One observer remarked during Assembly debates that "Galloway remarkably displayed his Talent of Eloquence & and extensive knowledge of the Laws of England and of ye fundamental principles of the British constitution and the judicial processes used in our Mother Country." Dickinson's biographer described Galloway as "a most brilliant lawyer. -- at the head of the bar."[16]

Unfortunately, the quality of apprenticeships varied with each law office. The extent of traditional emphasis on procedural matters generated most dispute. Admittedly, limited doses of this approach were justified. Knowledge of correct processes occasionally saved a new lawyer from destroying his tenuous reputation. Choosing an incorrect form of action might lead to disaster, regardless of the demands of justice, or a client. But the excesses of drudgery remained undisputed. For lack of time or too many students, sometimes through false pedagogy, attorneys often set their apprentices copying legal documents, "The trash of an office," Blackstone called it."[17]

The mass of critics complained that their training was overly endowed with irrelevance, that they wasted the prime of youth, then found themselves incompetent in middle age. So John Adams mentally berated his old teacher, Putnam, when he botched up his first "declaration in trespass for a rescue." He explained, "I never saw a writ in that law of the province. I was perplexed, and am very anxious about it. Now I feel the disadvantages of Putnam's insociability and neglect of me. Had he given me, now and then, a few hints concerning practice, I should be able to judge better at this hour than I can now. I have reason to complain of him," Adams concluded.[18]

The lack of books was a major colonial problem. Private libraries occasionally solved the book shortage, but more serious was the absence of American case reports, which crippled attempts to establish indigenous legal uniformity. Virginia had published an <u>Abridged Acts of Assembly</u> up to 1758; these reports then required additional private annotations. Not until 1801 did New York publish reports of court cases, which suffered from the verbosity of lawyers whose fees were set according to the bulk of their pleas.[19]

It is obvious, however, that not all colonial problems were uniquely colonial. On both sides of the Atlantic, lawyers craved training which would correlate theory and procedure, and give meaning to everyday practice. Their desire for order in the curriculum lured all students to cherish how-to pamphlets, as if these granted keys to the occult.

Some lawyers sympathetic to problems of undirected legal education drew up reading lists. Jefferson's were among the most detailed. His recommendations attempted to cover the broad sweep of knowledge he considered essential for a good lawyer. He suggested Montesquieu, Locke, Bolingbroke, Lord Kames, Blackstone, and Algernon Sidney, whose _Discourses Concerning. Government_ he described as "a rich treasure of republican principles, supported by copious and cogent arguments...it is probably the best elementary book of the principles of government, as founded on natural right...."[20] He added specific works on ancient history: Rollins, _Ancient History_. Livy, Plutarch's _Lives_, Vertot's _Revolutions of Rome_, and the political moralities of Thomas Gordon's translation of Sallust and Tacitus, of which he was particularly fond.[21] Jefferson did not neglect modern history, finding there many analogies to the past. He suggested Robertson's _History of Charles V_, and _History of Scotland._ Clarendon's _History of the Rebellion_, Bossuet's _History of France_, Keith's _History of Virginia_, and Stith's _History of Virginia_, for more indigenous application.

Others supported Jefferson's view. When William Smith of New York proposed a course of study for law students, he suggested three categories of legal knowledge, with appropriate books: general law -- Wood's _Institutes_ and Pufendorf's _Whole Duty of Man_;

common law -- Hale, Fortescue, Bacon, Wood on common law, Thomas Smith's de Republica Anglorum, and Doctor and Student; and the law of nature Pufendorf and Grotius.[22] Although not as ambitious as Jefferson, Smith's suggestions equally reflect assumptions of broad perspective as a prerequisite for the law, and more practically, required less than six years' study.

John Adams, who had bitterly complained about the amount of useless writ writing in his own training, also advised his students to concentrate on the broad impact of Coke, Plowden, Bracton, Britten, Fleta, and Glanville for common law, Justinian, Wood, and Domat for civil law, "interspersed with History, oratory, law, politics, and Warr and Commerce...."[23] These sources, and more, had been available to him in Gridley's library, a large segment of which he purchased in 1768 when Gridley died.[24]

Adams' reading program under Gridley's tutelage was impressive in scope. With fluctuating ardor, Adams spent two years seeking out, then rejecting law books. For civil law he waded through Johannes van Muyden's abridgement of Justinian's Institutes, borrowed from Gridley, and Thomas Wood's A New Institute of the Imperial or Civil Law.[25] He made a number of attempts to read Montesquieu's Spirit of the Laws, but found more pleasure in Hale's History of the Common Law. He borrowed the latter from Otis in the hope of comparing it with Blackstone, which he did a year later.[26] He also added Wood, Coke, Salkeld's Reports, Hawkins' Pleas of the Crown, Fortescue, Pufendorf, and Grotius to his pedagogical burdens.[27]

Alexander Hamilton's preparations in the law provides similar evidence of broad perspectives. Although he officially studied for only six months, he had use of James Duane's library, the "best" in Albany.[28] His speed is understandable in view of his earlier preparation at King's College. There he had read Burlamaqui, Grotius, Locke, Montesquieu, Pufendorf and Blackstone, before going on to more technical studies.[29] In his first political pamphlet, _The Farmer Refuted_, a rejoinder to Samuel Seabury's _A View of the Constitution_, Hamilton made ample use of his readings. His citations frequently pointed to Grotius, Pufendorf, Locke, Montesquieu, Burlamaqui, Hobbes, Blackstone, and _Calvin's Case_ as materials for his arguments.[30]

These colonial lawyers prepared for the law along patterns reminiscent of the best in English traditions. They made it evident that high achievement by colonists was not impossible; neither was it impossible for the mediocre to pass through. The problem lay on the disparity of standards set by local groups whose spasmodic attempts at controls failed to deal with general mediocrity.

Not only did standards vary from colony to colony, but within a colony the criteria for local evaluating boards differed, as well. When John Adams left Putnam in Worcester for Gridley and Pratt in Braintree, Pratt advised Adams to obtain references from Putnam, but Gridley cryptically advised that he "get sworn" as the first step toward mastering legal practice. Gridley offered to recommend Adams to the Court, "then Mr. Prat said 2 or 3 Words, and the clerk was ordered to swear us."[31]

On other occasions a board would change its standards as the applicants changed. Patrick Henry aroused Jefferson's ire for many reasons, among which was Henry's admission to the bar after an undetermined period of study lasting somewhere between six weeks and six months. The accounts of the examination vary in some details, but essentially Henry proved himself a skillful manipulator of legal theory, and the examiners decided he would learn procedure after he, too, "got sworn."[32]

Sporadic attempts to improve professional standards sometimes resulted from base reasons. As did their English counterparts, colonial lawyers sought to regulate the number and social status of their law clerks by quotas and high fees; they hoped to prevent a competitive glut on the market and an onslaught by the venturesome poor. In 1756, the New York bar set a high 200 pound fee for apprentices.[33] For the same restrictive reasons, they attempted to institute a fourteen-year moratorium on the training of all clerks, except their own sons. At the end of the moratorium period each lawyer would be permitted to have one clerk at a time, and only such persons could be sponsored for admission to the bar. Within a decade the impossibility of enforcing the moratorium became apparent, although they did attempt a two-clerk limitation for reasons of supply and demand.[34] Similar activity occurred in

Massachusetts. During the March term of 1768, the Essex County bar proposed restrictions also designed to curtail the increasing attractiveness of the legal profession. It would seem that time had alleviated the shortage of lawyers which once forced them to swear that one client could not monopolize the services of more than two lawyers per case. By 1768, the danger of oversupply prompted a measure restricting lawyers to those new clerks approved by the bar, and these had to pay 100 pound sterling for their training.[35]

Additional prestige-enhancing procedures included select societies, regular meetings, and grants of neo-English titles. In New York, in 1770, twelve influential lawyers officially, though vainly, organized themselves to debate important issues, and to discuss technical questions in law.[36] The board of Essex County, Massachusetts, established criteria of seniority to recreate artificial replicas of English attorneys and barristers. The former became the latter after two years practice in the Superior court, which, in turn, presupposed three years' study with another barrister (later modified by the Suffolk bar to permit study with an attorney), and two years practice in an Inferior Court.[37] John Adams reported that as a result of Chief Justice Hutchinson's attempt to establish judicial dignity, he wore "Gowns and Bands and tye Wiggs" upon becoming a barrister.[38] In January, 1770, Boston barristers and attorneys met at the Bunch of Grapes Tavern on State and Kilby Streets to form a secret "society or law club" to meet the first Wednesday of every month. The club's secretary was John Adams and included James Otis, Samuel Quincy, Daniel Leonard, Francis Dana, and Josiah Quincy. But as the records for February and march were to show, response by the pseudo-collaborators proved to be "thin"."[39]

American lawyers, like their English counterparts, spent much of their professional time, as Adams put it, "fumbling and raking amidst the rubbish of writs, indightments, Pleas, ejectments, enfiefed, illaterbration and a 1000 other lignum vitae words that have neither harmony nor meaning."[40] As in England, colonial lawyers were valued for the techniques at their disposal, feared for the prosperity which seemed to result, and maligned for the pettiness and drudgery ascribed to their days and, ultimately, to their lives. Indeed, were it not for the legal change of pace offered by imperial problems prior to the American Revolution, there is no evidence to indicate that any would have deviated from that which some found a "slavish practice."[41]

The "bread and butter" cases of professional lawyers consisted of routine suits for debts and other technical business. John Adams' legal papers indicate that his cases revolved around commercial transactions -- promissory notes, bonds, agreements between Bostonian and European merchants --local regulations, and the eternally consistent cases -- murder, rape, larceny, assault, counterfeiting, rioting, mobbing, and the localized incidents of tarring and feathering. In short, he met a cross-section of

Massachusetts society.[42] No different, either, were the records or John Jay, James Otis, Sr., or Alexander Hamilton.[43]

Nor did cases vary significantly on geographic grounds. In the twelve years Thomas Jefferson practiced law, he, too, coped with trespass, injury to property, theft, wills, estates, assault and battery, and family quarrels. Land litigation for eminent Virginia families composed the bulk of his work, as would be expected, but he also devoted a great deal of legal energy to British firms, either collecting for them or defending against them.[44] So, too, did Patrick Henry, whose fee books show that the major portion of his work consisted of collecting debts for merchants.[45] Records show he also dabbled in the sale of Negroes, a case involving the "unlawful use of gelding," and slander (his client had been called a "hog stealer"), as well as traditionally technical business.[46]

Clients perennially and fervently conjured up a great wealth presumably extorted from them by their counsel. Some of the malevolence can be ascribed to normal illwill toward creditors. Yet recent studies substantiate allegations of upward mobility through law. Jackson Turner Main argues that although there were gradations in wealth, the law was the most profitable of all professions."[47] Cadwallader Colden had remarked similarly in 1765, when he drew up categories of colonial rank in which he placed members of the bench and bar second only to the proprietors of the great landed estates.[48]

Colonial lawyers with prestige, proper connections, good timing, a profitable location, and persistence, might achieve great wealth, which was America's dream. Statistics which suggest economic opportunity for lawyers also reveal other aspects of legal life in America. They reveal that although in most cases a reputable lawyer could establish and maintain solvency tinged with affluence via his law practice, the relative wealth of many stemmed from other factors.

Among the examples of prosperity Main cites is James Allen of Pennsylvania. Main points to Allen's 300-400 pound income as of 1773, a figure Allen substantiated in his Diary. and adds that in two years that income doubled.[49] Unmentioned was the possibility that this increase, as well as Allen's total annual revenue of 1,000 pounds stemmed from kinship to Chief Justice William Allen, or Andrew Hamilton, the Attorney-General of Pennsylvania, or Governor James Hamilton, or the prestige of study at the Inns of Court. The rewards were subtle. But grouse hunting with the secretary of the land office might bag a variety of returns.[50]

William Allen's speculative interests were closely tied to his law practice. For example, in 1753 he attempted to purchase land belonging to clients of a London attorney. These clients owned eight thousand acres of "unlocated land." Allen wrote that the claim was losing value; good lands were either taken by squatters or purchased by the proprietor. Allen advised: "if care is taken by persons well acquainted in the County, some good lands may be got. But if the Heirs of the Family do not sell before that time, or get some very judicious person immediately after it to locate their lands....their Rights will be of no value....if they keep their Lands another twenty years in their Hands, the whole 8000 acres will not be worth Fifty Guineas."[51] Allen offered them 800 pounds.

Similar evidence of secondary resources were found in other records. Thomas Jefferson's yearly income during his twelve-year practice averaged $3,000, although his fees were moderate and the number of his cases varied from 115 in 1768 to 400 in 1771.[52] Here not only landed interests but pre-revolutionary ferment may have contributed to his greater popularity. Certainly, the Revolution saved the career of William Paterson. Paterson began practice in 1769 in Hunterdon County, New Jersey, with a good record for winning 69% of his cases, when he could get them. In his first three years he approximated two cases per quarter session of the local court, and by 1774 he was also running a country store in Princeton.[53] Revolutionary activity was to place a premium on his legal skills, otherwise left unnoticed.

Among the ordinary obstacles to wealth against which lawyers did battle was the legislated proscription against exorbitant fees. While designed primarily to hamper charlatans, it frequently strained the resources of more vulnerable colonial lawyers. An example of the former was Thomas Macnemora of Maryland. Macnemora was suspended from practice for charging a pauper entitled to free counsel fees of 12 shillings and 100 pounds of bacon.[54] The statutes on fees were passed to set rates for cases in the judicial hierarchy, to which lawyers responded in a multitude of ways. Some insisted on down-payments before walking into court.[55] Others began to emphasize quantity as a path to wealth. Some have suggested that the litigiousness of New Englanders was the result of law fees and the need of lawyers to maintain a heavy portfolio.[56]

Large numbers of simple cases could be had by riding circuit. James Otis., Sr., of whom the tactless John Adams remarked, "learned he is not." commanded half the practice in Braintree County, and rode circuit in addition, sometimes bringing suits against his own clients for non-payment. He required an extensive practice, since he charged only fifteen to twenty shillings per action. Within a decade he was earning 1,200 pounds yearly.[57] Riding circuit, one could obtain cases at the courthouse door. By riding quickly, one could obtain many cases. John Adams peevishly wrote of Josiah Quincy, Jr., in 1774, that "he would not stop, but drove forward, I suppose that he might get upon the Fishing Ground before his Brother Sam, and me."[58] Adams, himself, more than matched their case numbers.[59] He reached his peak between 1768 and 1773, when imperial matters began to distract. By then he had become the "busiest lawyer" in Braintree County.[60]

Some lawyers chose to settle in the hinterlands because of the limited competition and the numerous clamoring clients. Half-way through the eighteenth century one could still have established a profitable urban practice without external support. Samuel Fitch, in 1750, was advised to practice in Boston because the eminent lawyers were "either Dead or incapable of doing much business."[61] And George Read was told by Moland to avoid the countryside, meaning Newcastle, because the local poverty was unprofitable for lawyers, and it was not fit for any person (to) live in....." Furthermore, leaving Philadelphia would deprive him of important contacts.[62] Such did not remain the case. James Wilson was to move to Carlisle for the abundance of litigation and the absence of competition. He soon cornered half the cases in Common Pleas.[63] Hugh Henry Brackenridge, a Scotsman, graduate of Princeton in 1771, and student of Samuel Chase, decided to practice in Pittsburgh to avoid the Philadelphia competition of Benjamin Chew, John Dickinson, and the established James Wilson.[64]

Among the advantages of frontier law practice, then, were the prospects of monopoly and the chance to learn one's trade. Frontier courts provided an informal atmosphere which frequently threw together self-trained justices (prone to right, if not precise, thinking), prestigious circuit riders, and fledgling lawyers, all in the great equality of local taverns. For example, in 1771, when the Pennsylvania courts extended their jurisdiction to include Bedford County and established the township of Pitt, the judges proved the "affinity between the Courts and the taverns...."[65] Westmoreland's first court was to be found in Robert Hanna's tavern; and the Allegheny County Court met on the third floor (a dangerous spot) of William Irwin's bar, but later moved to John Reed's "Sign of the Waggon."[66]

The laxity of all but the highest courts resulted from the abundance of untrained judges. But these could not have monopolized judicial seats had trained lawyers not rebelled against accepting less-lucrative judicial posts. Occasionally lack of social standing or property, or some obstacle of political allegiance prevented appointment of a lawyer willing to take a judicial appointment.[67] In 1770, Lieutenant-Governor Bull suggested to the Earl of Hillsborough that he send overage English lawyers whose limited prospects of success would make them eager to accept the American appointment, "where their advancing age would be cherished by our mild climate, giving dignity to their office, and authority to their decision"[68] Fortunately, these pastured officials remained dependent upon English sufferance. It was not until uniformity of training among American lawyers made an equally well-trained judiciary vital that salaries and talent of judges began to approach professional standards.

As John Adams indicated, professionalism for colonial lawyers required a variety of talents, some unique to America: familiarity with the broad perspective of the ancient constitution and the lessons of English and continental history, and a firm grasp of the technique of procedure with which philosophy became practice. Unlike the English, colonial lawyers struggled also with fitting English practice to a semi-urban and frontier environment. In a sense, that transfer demanded commonplacing on a grand scale; the process of selection depended upon great insight into the functions of everyday procedure.[69] It was not until the end of the French and Indian War, however, that another dimension was added to the legal perspective. The new imperial policy which followed the war shifted emphasis in the colonies from routine practice to the principles of imperial relations: how did ties between England and the colonies fit in the ancient constitution? That problem was to occupy colonial lawyers until 1776. In Pennsylvania, colonial lawyers were granted a preview of the imperial perspective when, from 1759 to 1764, they worked to exchange their proprietary charter for a royal. That debate brought John Dickinson, fresh from the Inns of Court, and Joseph Galloway, their first taste of the imperial dilemma.

Footnotes

[1] Richard B. Morris, "Legalism *versus* Revolutionary Doctrine in New England," *New England Quarterly* (1931), 195: Daniel Boorstin, *The Americans, The Colonial Experience* (New York, 1964), 195-205.

[2] George Lee Haskins, *Law and Authority in Early Massachusetts, A Study in Tradition and Design* (New York, 1960), 2, 6-7, 106, 119, 147. Also see Haskins, "A Problem in the Reception of the Common Law in the Colonial Period," *University of Pennsylvania Law Review* (1949), 842-53: Julius Goebel, "King's Law and Local Custom in Seventeenth Chancery New England," *Columbia Law Review* (1931), 416-17, 420-21; Stanley Katz takes a position similar to that of Haskins and Goebel in a review article, "Looking Backward: The Early History of American Law," *University of Chicago Law Review* (1966), 870-72; Goebel, ed., *The Law Practice of Alexander Hamilton, Documents and Commentary* (New York, 1964). 9-11.

[3] In 1765 Cadwallader Colden wrote to the Earl of Halifax to describe the symbiotic landed-political-legal complex which dominated New York. See Irving Mark, *Agrarian Conflicts in Colonial New York, 1711-1775* (New York, 1940), 85.

[4] Adams, *Diary*, I, 55.

[5] Roscoe Pound, *The Lawyer from Antiquity to Modern Times*...(Minnesota, 1953), 158-60.

[6] Burton Alva Konkle, *Benjamin Chew, 1722-1810* (Philadelphia, 1932), 46-47.

[7] Ibid., 38-39.

[8] H. Trevor Colbourn, ed., "A Pennsylvania Farmer at the Court of King George, John Dickinson's London Letters, 1754-1756," Pennsylvania Magazine of History and Biography (1962), 257 (hereafter cited as London Letters).

[9] Ibid., 257-58.

[10] Ibid., 259.

[11] Ibid., 249.

[12] Ibid., 267.

[13] Ibid., 269.

[14] Quoted in Francis D. Wormuth, Origins of Modern Constitutionalism (New York, 1949), 169. Residence requirements at the Inns of Court were met by dining in the halls three times a term for five years, paying fees, and passing through pro-forma ceremonies. See Sir William Holdsworth, A History of English Law (London, 1938), XII, 79; W.T. Loftie, The Inns of Court and Chancery (London, 1895), 102-04! F.A. Inderwick, ed., A Calendar of the Inner Temple Records (London, 1901), III, lxiii, 25: Paul Q. Hamlin, Legal Education in Colonial New York (New York, 1939), 16.

[15] Clifford K. Shipton, ed., Sibley's Harvard Graduates. Biographical Sketches of those who Attended Harvard (Boston, 1960), VII, 523.

[16] Stille, Dickinson, 117: Samuel Foulke, "The Pennsylvania Assembly in 1761-2. A Memorandum Kept by Samuel Foulke," PMHB.

VIII (1884), 410.

[17] Blackstone, Commentaries, I, 32. 18 Charles Francis Adams, ed., The Works of John Adams (Boston, 1856), II, 52 (hereafter cited as Adams, Works).

[18] Charles Francis Adams, ed., The Works of John Adams (Boston, 1856), II, 52 (hereafter cited as Adams, Works).

[19] Malone, Jefferson, 70: Goebel, Hamilton Papers, Preface, x.

[20] Sowerby, III, 12.

[21] Ibid., I, 37-38.

[22] Hamlin, Legal Education, Appendix viii, 197-200: Dorothy Rita Dillon, The New York Triumvirate, A Study of the Legal and Political Careers of William Livingston. John Morin Scott, William Smith, Jr. (New York, 1949), 241.

[23] L. Kinvin Wroth and Hiller B. Zobel, ed., Legal Papers of John Adams (New York, 1968), I, lxxxiii (hereafter cited as Adams, Legal Papers).

[24] Ibid., lxxv-vi.

[25] L. H. Butterfield, ed., The Earliest Diary of John Adams. June 1753-April 1754, Sept. 1758-January 1759 (Cambridge, 1966), 55-58: Adams, Diary. 163.

[26] Ibid., I, 142, 169, 225.

[27] Ibid., 173-74.

[28] Goebel, Hamilton Papers, 48-49.

[29] Ibid., 9.

[30] Alexander Hamilton, "The Farmer Refuted," in Harold C. Syrett, ed., *The Papers of Alexander Hamilton* (New York, 1961), 86-142, *passim*.

[31] Adams, *Diary.* I, 54-59.

[32] Robert D. Meade, *Patrick Henry, Patriot in the Making* (Philadelphia and New York, 1957), 95-97.

[33] Hamlin, *Legal Education*. 37-39.

[34] *Ibid*., 160, 163.

[35] George Dexter, ed., "Record Book of the Suffolk Bar, 1770-1805" Massachusetts Historical Society, *Proceedings*, XIX (1881-82), 142-43, 154 (hereafter cited as Dexter, *Suffolk Bar*).

[36] Dillon, *Triumvirate.* 25-26; Frank Monaghan, *John Jay: Defender of Liberty Against Kings and Peoples* (New York, 1935), 42.

[37] Dexter, *Suffolk Bar.* 147, 150.

[38] Adams, *Legal Papers.* I, lviii.

[39] Dexter, *Suffolk Bar.* 147-48.

[40] Adams, *Legal Papers*, I, iii.

[41] Franklin B. Dexter, ed., *A Selection from the Correspondence of Jared Ingersoll*. New Haven Colonial Society, IX (1918), April 14, 1764.

[42] Adams, *Legal Papers*, I, lx.

[43] Monaghan, *John Jay.* 45; Goebel, *Hamilton Papers*, xi; John Waters, Jr., *Otis Family in Provincial and Revolutionary*

Massachusetts (Chapel Hill, 1968), 68.

[44] Gilbert Chinard, Thomas Jefferson, The Apostle of Americanism (Boston, 1929). 36.

[45] Clement Eaton, "Mirror of a Southern Colonial Lawyer" The Fee Books of Patrick Henry, Thomas Jefferson, and Waightsill Avery," William and Mary Quarterly, VIII (1951), 524-26 (hereafter cited as WMQ).

[46] Meade, Patrick Henry. 77, 99-101.

[47] Jackson Turner Main, The Social Structure of Revolutionary America (Princeton, 1965), 101, 113, 192.

[48] Quoted in Mark, Agrarian Conflicts, 85.

[49] Main, Social Structure, 101: "Diary of James Allen Esq., of Philadelphia, Counsellor-at-Law, 1770-1778," PMHB, IX (1885), Oct. 30, 1773.

[50] Ibid., 176-78.

[51] William Allen to Evans Patterson, Nov. 5' 1753, in Lewis Burd Walker, ed., Extracts from Letterbook (n.p., 1897), 6-7.

[52] Chinard, Jefferson, 36.

53 Richard C. Haskett, "William Paterson, Attorney General of New Jersey, Public Office and Private Profit in the American Revolution," WMQ. vii (1950), 26-27.

[54] Aubrey C. Land, The Dulanys of Maryland, A Biographical Study of Daniel Dulany, the Elder (1685-1753) and Daniel Dulany, the Younger (1722-1797), Studies in Maryland History, no. 3 (Baltimore, 1955), 8, 33.

[55] Jefferson, Papers, I, 98-99.

[56] Sibley, Harvard Graduates. VII, 521.

[57] Waters, Otis, 69, 72.

[58] Adams, Legal Papers. I, lxix.

[59] Adams, Diary, I, 136, 138.

[60] Adams, Legal Papers, I, lviii.

61 Quoted in Sibley, Harvard Graduates, XI, 144.

[62] William Thompson Read, Life and Correspondence of George Read (Philadelphia, 1870), 12-13.

[63] Smith, James Wilson. 44.

[64] Thomas R. Meehan, "Courts, Cases, and Counselors in Revolutionary and Post-Revolutionary Pennsylvania," PMHB, XLI (1967), 22.

[65] A. B. Reid, "Early Courts, Judges, and Lawyers of Allegheny County," Western Pennsylvania Historical Magazine, V (1922), 186.

[66] Ibid.

[67] Paul M. Hamlin and Charles E Baker, Supreme Court of Judicature of the Province of New York, 1691-1704 (New York Historical Society, 1952). 83-85.

[68] Leonard Wood Labaree, Royal Government in America, A Study of the British Colonial System before 1783 (New Haven, 1930), 364.

[69] John Adams' Pleadings Book, in which he catalogued forms of action, is a case in point. In it, he narrowed down procedure to basic forms, using simplicity and speed as his criteria. See Adams, Legal Papers, I, 26-86.

CHAPTER THREE

CHARTER CRISIS IN PENNSYLVANIA, 1759-1764

In 1764, and again in 1776, Pennsylvania faced an internal constitutional crisis. In both instances the issue was the disposition of social and political power within the colony. In 1764, many in the Assembly favored exchanging the proprietary charter under which the colony had lived since 1701 for royal government, in order to eliminate the proprietor's political control of the colony. That venture was interrupted, however, by the larger events of 1765 to 1775. The prospect of independence in 1775 reopened the latent struggle. Those who considered themselves disfranchised by the Assembly's political structure saw in independence from Great Britain a way to unseat the moderate whigs hitherto controlling that body. In Pennsylvania, independence became inextricably tied to the constitution of 1776. John Dickinson, who supported the proprietary charter in 1764 continued to support it in 1776, both on its own merits and because he opposed the assertion of independence implicit in the new constitution's preamble.[1] James Wilson joined Dickinson on this issue; although he finally signed the Declaration of Independence, Wilson strongly opposed the new constitution in Pennsylvania. It must also be pointed out that the discontented frontiersmen who supported the proprietary in 1764 against the Assembly were the same men who supported independence and the new constitutional structure.

The intricacies of these issues are important, then, for two reasons, first the social forces which caused the constitutional issue in 1776 first emerged in the heat of the charter conflict a dozen years earlier; second, they provided early insight into the constitutional views of Joseph Galloway and John Dickinson on issues which foreshadowed the revolutionary debates. Because of these ties between the preliminary crisis in Pennsylvania and crises of revolution and independence, we need to take a closer look at Pennsylvania's internal structure.

The essential constitutional question in Pennsylvania during the eighteenth century concerned the prerogatives guaranteed the Assembly by the original grant and the later charter privileges of 1701, which they had forced from their proprietor.[2] In the fashion of provincial assemblies in the eighteenth century, the lower house claimed all the prerogatives gained by the House of Commons in the Glorious Revolution, which, of course, the proprietors refused to allow. As a result, seemingly parochial issues -- proprietary instructions to the governor, Indian policy, currency questions, Quaker "pacifism," and proper defense against the French and Indians took on greater significance than these questions otherwise would warrant. Joseph Galloway and Benjamin Franklin emerged as the Assembly's political spokesmen in opposition to the proprietor's men, with whom John Dickinson appeared to be allied.

Already the great issues of revolution had been joined: parliamentary supremacy and the role of discretionary power over the colonies. Although Pennsylvanians did not yet know it (they separated the interests of the proprietor from those of the Crown) the Assembly's attempt to redress the balance of proprietary and local power was viewed in England as an attack upon imperial authority and as disloyalty during the war for empire. Within a decade it was to become obvious that the issue was between the colonies and Parliament. For the moment, the proprietor's role beclouded that perception. Pennsylvanians believed the Crown to be their ally.[3]

For the Quakers, the Assembly had become the prime political weapon with which to balance the proprietary power. But they could no longer rely on their numbers alone to assure hegemony of that body. For a time, they successfully conspired to manipulate political representation. Of the thirty-six members, the predominately Quaker counties of Philadelphia, Chester, and Bucks controlled twenty-six seats. Of the frontier counties, Berks and Northampton had one vote each, Lancaster had four, and Cumberland and York received two each. Until 1776, when the Quakers suffered public defeat, the Assembly contained sixteen Quakers, eleven Anglicans, six Ulster Presbyterians, one Lutheran, one Moravian, and one Baptist.[4] The Quakers could also rely on the support of the

Germans, who sympathized with Quaker pacifism.

The proprietors, on the other side, brought to the battle support from many quarters. In the natural course of events the proprietary could rely upon the influence generated by charter rights, prestige and patronage. The proprietor issued secret and binding instructions to his governor in which he set policy and limitations upon the governor's power to compromise. (The Assembly vehemently opposed those instructions as an unconstitutional limit to their legislative initiative.) In the proprietor's name the governor could also exercise veto rights and use his influence upon a subservient council to manipulate (in theory) the activities of freemen in the Assembly. Parenthetically, it should be pointed out that the Crown supported proprietary privileges as an extension of its own battle against legislative incursions.

The Penns also won support for economic reasons. Many councilors received monopolies of choice political offices which inevitably resulted in great opportunities for wealth.[5]

The resentments of the Scotch-Irish Presbyterians provided the proprietors with a third source of potential power against the Quakers. Insecurity marked the lives of the Scotch-Irish. They had arrived in the 1730s, and since then, they had squatted on frontier lands to which they had no title. Threatened and threatening Indians viewed the frontiersmen's expansion as symbolic of the white man's menace. While the Indians vented their antagonisms on the unprotected farmers, the Quaker pacifists who controlled the Assembly refused to hear pleas for defensive measures. To the Scotch-Irish, the Quakers represented the authority which deprived them of land, defense, and representation. They looked to the proprietary as the only alternative to the Assembly.

The battlefield took this form: the Quakers, on one side, controlled the Assembly as a result of the charter of 1701. The charter granted to the Assembly full prerogatives, guaranteed freedom of religion, and abolished test oaths. For the remainder of the charter's life, the Assembly upheld it as a symbol of a popular victory over oppression, as a defense against further onslaughts by the proprietary, and as encouragement to continued vigilance. Ideologically, assemblymen perceived themselves as staunch defenders of legislative rights against opponents in London. Ironically, they were finally willing to give up their charter in order to preserve it.[6] All the jockeying for position that marred proprietary interchange with the Assembly reflected the development of a hardening political stance on both sides. Assembly stalwarts argued that the proprietor's rights lived on as an anachronistic reminder of a Stuart power which had been destroyed by the Glorious Revolution. Quakers further claimed that if Stuart tyranny no longer bound England, it should not flourish in Pennsylvania. They and the Assembly must insure the political leverage with which to secure colonial rights and maintain the political equality of all Englishmen.

In the Spring of 1755, Isaac Norris II, a leading Pennsylvania Quaker who became Dickinson's father-in-law, wrote a letter to a London Friend in which he claimed, " we have very much thrown our Disputes from being a Quaker cause, to a Cause of Liberty, and the Rights derived to us by our Charter and our Laws."[7] Events ultimately proved Norris right. But the more immediate impact of their efforts was to arouse the opposition to a consolidated campaign to politically eradicate the Quakers.

Thus, in March, 1756, the inevitable happened. A report to the privy council concluded that "There is no Reason to hope that proper or effectual Measures will be taken, while the Majority of the Assembly consists of Persons whose avowed Principles are against military Services, however necessary for the Security and Defense of Government...."[8] The report suggested remedial legislation. These ill-winds soon reached the Quakers. Rumor had it that the Board of Trade would require test oaths of all office-holders. The London Friends began sending frantic warnings to the Philadelphia Quakers that abdication would be officially imposed upon them unless they voluntarily resigned their seats. Therefore, in June 1756, six orthodox Quakers left the Assembly, and four other Quakers refused office after the October elections.[9] Franklin commented, "The Quakers have now pretty generally declined their Seats in the Assembly, very few remaining. We shall soon see if Matters will be better managed by a Majority of different religious Persuasions."[10]

In the summer of 1755, Franklin abandoned his sometimes pro-proprietary, sometimes neutral position, to join the Quakers as their political ally. Franklin's influence was thought by the proprietary to be so pervasive that in 1775 Governor Morris insisted that he had played Pygmalion to the Assembly's Galatea.[11] In fact, Franklin's power base was with the Norrisites, that group led by the Assembly's speaker, Isaac Norris, who believed in the need for political participation. Israel Pemberton, clerk of the Pennsylvania and New Jersey Meeting, led a dissident faction which emphasized the strict tenets of Quakerism, and this group opposed Franklin. There is good evidence to suggest that Franklin's break with Thomas Penn resulted from a challenge to his convictions, specifically, publication of the proprietor's instructions to control dispersal of appropriations, which Franklin characterized as a violation of the Assembly's "natural Exclusive Right," and Penn's refusal to permit taxation of his estates after Braddock's death. The Rev. William Smith recounted that Franklin "originally crept into confidence under the character of a <u>common wealth's man</u> with the cry of our constitution and <u>charter rights</u> in his mouth." And in the summer of 1756, Governor Morris wrote William Shirley of Franklin's "very out of the way notions of the power of the People," and added that he was "as much a favourer of the unreasonable claims of American assemblies as any man whatever."[12]

The union of Franklin and Quaker political acumen proved very effective. Franklin brought with him the influence of one who had a printed forum, and the Quakers contributed an informal electoral system which they directed from their meetinghouse.[13] The immediate results could be seen in the election of 1756. Although many Quakers had resigned, they remained in position to nominate and elect non-Quakers who sympathized with their philosophical views. Among these nominees was Joseph Galloway.[14]

Galloway soon proved an effective lieutenant in the new political alliance. Penn's supporter, the Rev. Richard Peters, described Galloway, the "young noisy Quaker member of the Law," as one of the "veriest partisans against the Proprietaries and moderate measures as could be picked out in this town."[15] Within a year of his election Galloway joined Norris and Franklin on the Assembly's committee to protest their grievances against tho proprietor and, when Franklin pursued the task to England, he left Galloway in control of the anti-proprietary group and charged the newcomer with defense of his reputation.[16] Within a decade Galloway rose to become speaker of the Assembly.

From 1757 to 1764, Franklin devoted his efforts to rectifying the constitutional imbalance he perceived in his adopted colony. The Pennsylvania Assembly directed Franklin and Isaac Norris to present their grievances to the crown and proprietors in the hope of changing proprietary instructions; the Assembly thought Franklin particularly skillful in the essential art of argumentation. Galloway was among those responsible for drawing up the list of grievances, and his influence was obvious in the final report, called the "Heads of Complaint."[17]

In the petition, the essential disagreement between Assembly and proprietor focused on the Assembly's authority and the validity of the constitution of 1701. The Assembly claimed in their report that they possessed "an original Right of Legislation inherent in them, which neither the Proprietaries, nor any other Person whatsoever can divest them of, restrain or abridge, without manifestly violating and destroying the letter, Spirit and Design of this Grant," an argument which Galloway developed in his own writings.[18] Another Galloway touch is found in the assertion that proprietary instructions interfered with charter rights of Assembly and governor to legislate "according to their best discretion."[19] The proprietors, however, dismissed the Assembly's aspirations. They asserted that the original royal charter superseded any concessions made by their father, and the charter from Charles II deliberately limited popular rights. Isaac Norris earlier had warned Franklin that the proprietor's agents "declare openly enough those Charters confirm to the people such Rights as are indeed necessary for a new Settlement but ought to be abridged upon the first favourable Occasion that offers...."[20] But when Franklin finally heard these sentiments from the proprietors, he was unprepared. Nor was he prepared for the assertion by Lord Granville that the king, rather than the Assembly, legislated for the colonies.[21]

The Assembly's move toward confrontation with the proprietors brought about the great debate between Galloway and John Dickinson. Some of their mutual antagonism can be explained on personal grounds. Both men sought political power in the Pennsylvania Assembly. By 1760, Galloway had distinguished himself as a lawyer, and he had become Franklin's lieutenant in the Assembly. When Dickinson returned from the Inns of Court, both the established lawyer and the newcomer found themselves before the supreme court, alternately confederates and opponents. In 1760, Dickinson was elected to the Delaware Assembly and became its speaker. Two years later, Dickinson and Galloway were elected to the Pennsylvania Assembly from the country of Philadelphia, and Dickinson began parcelling out his growing law practice to others. He assured his mother in 1763 that "money flows in, and my Vanity has been agreeably flattered of late...."[22] In the Assembly he received committee assignments that gradually brought him to the attention of his fellows. The two men found themselves in situations ripe with potential for personal antagonism which they finally expressed in the heat of debate over Pennsylvania's constitution.[23]

Although the exchange between Dickinson and Galloway is labelled a "debate," Galloway made a much more lucid statement of his ideas in a pamphlet written in 1759, called "A True and Impartial State of the Province of Pennsylvania," in which he countered the charges made by William Smith some four years previous."[24]

The Reverend William Smith, Anglican provost of the College

of Philadelphia, wrote a pamphlet in 1755, called "A Brief State of the Province of Pennsylvania," clarifying the half-century of conflict between the Assembly and the proprietor.[25] He answered the question: "why we, who are esteemed one of the richest Colonies in North America, are the most backward in contributing to the Defense of the British Dominion in these Parts, against...the French.?"[26] Smith responded predictably by blaming the Assembly, Quaker-controlled and grown inflexible in old age. In Smith's and the proprietor's eyes, the Assembly had also grown too powerful. Underlying the complaints of inadequate defense were charges that the Assembly pretended to "Extraordinary" power based on their charter of 1701.[27]

Galloway's response deserves more attention than it has received because it synthesized the Assembly's constitutional arguments, but more importantly it revealed Galloway's personal constitutional philosophy, one to which he was to remain faithful for the remainder of his political life.

The core of Galloway's constitutional thinking is found in the "Nature of Powers": power viewed as an indivisible whole. Power had been made legitimate in the British constitution by its correct apportionment between king, lords, and commons in Parliament (according to their natural functions) in the revolution of 1688. Each body had received powers which were essential to its integrity. The "nature of powers" was such that neither crown, nor commons, nor subjects, could permit infringements upon the power or functions of one without destroying the mutual dependence upon which harmonious operations relied. Of the many virtues of the English constitution not the least was the balance which provided that "his Majesty's private Interest and Welfare are inseparably connected with, and dependent on the Prosperity of his People."[28]

Pursuing a similar theme, Galloway believed that the colonists had carried with them the rights of Englishmen. In his dedication to William Pitt, he proclaimed:

> Men of the highest Estimation for Virtue and Learning have declared, that no Change of Climate, no distance of Places.can destroy, or even abridge those Rights and Privileges, which a Briton derives from his Nativity. They are Blessings that inseparably went on his Person, in all his Migrations and Settlement.

From these assumptions, based on the "Principles of Reason and natural Equity," Galloway went on to conclude that the collective political body in the colony, the Pennsylvania Assembly, possessed the powers claimed by the collective political body in England, the House of Commons."[29]

The powers of the Pennsylvania Assembly were further reinforced by the authority of the crown. According to Galloway's interpretation, the charter from Charles II had vested the original rights of legislation in the people's representatives. The provision in question granted legislative power "to...William Penn and his Heirs.." to ordain, make and enact, and under his and their seals to publish any Laws whatsoever....according to their best Discretion, by and with the Advice, Consent, and Approbation of the Freemen...or of their Delegates or Deputies...."[30] Galloway's reading here is typically whiggish. By shifting the object of "according to their best Discretion," he modernized the document to give a power to the people never envisioned by Charles II. Newly interpreted through whig glasses, that provision then read that "the Deputies and Lieutenant of William Penn, and his Heirs, were to concur with the People. in framing Laws, according to their best Discretion."[31]

Galloway had great faith in Pennsylvania's constitution. Montesquieu thought William Penn a modern Lycurgus, and Galloway agreed.[32] The proprietor and people ostensibly had contrived a constitution "equally adapted to preserve the just Prerogatives of the Crown, and the Rights and Liberties of the Subject, and nearly resembling that of the Mother Country."[33] Galloway's reinterpretation of the charter implied that both the subjects and the proprietary had the right to choose representatives in the legislature. But once chosen, those representatives, in accordance with the "nature of powers," became an entity possessing "the whole Power of their Principles." Galloway claimed that the office and the power were one and united,

> that they cannot be constituted to do a single Act, or to execute of Office of their Constituents in Part only. Nor can their Power be diminished by any Covenant or Bond. given to their Principles. For should they covenant, not to do any particular Act, which their Constituents might do, such Covenant is repugnant, and void in Law....[34]

Galloway further claimed that in 1724, Hannah Penn, widow of the proprietor, had admitted "that the Powers of the Legislature are lodged solely in the Governor and Assembly, without as much as a Negative reserved in the Proprietary, if absent."[35]

On that premise Galloway logically concluded that the proprietors consistently and deliberately engaged in activities designed to undermine the constitutional guarantees bestowed by the crown and the charter of 1701.[36]

He charged, for example, that William Smith and his patrons violated the constitution's guarantees of religious freedom when they encouraged test oaths for office-holders.[37] And he charged that the proprietors attempted to deprive the Assembly of the privileges belonging to the House of Commons, "and consequently the Rights of the Assembly of Pennsylvania...according to the Rights of Freeborn Subjects of England."[38] He also charged that the proprietors threatened the rights of Englishmen by imposing a militia law to which the Assembly objected not merely as Quakers but "as Subjects."[39] They feared, he wrote, that an established militia would inevitably open a new patronage system independent of the Assembly and reliant only upon the governor.

The patronage issue affected the judiciary as well. In England, the Act of Settlement of 1701 had established judicial Tenure during Good behavior instead of "during the king's pleasure," in order to ensure judicial independence. The change had not been applicable to the colonies. In 1754, new instructions specifically insisted on judicial tenure "during pleasure alone." In 1759, the privy council disallowed Pennsylvania legislation to make judicial tenure permanent and thereby less susceptible to proprietary influence. Since the Assembly already controlled judicial salaries, the proprietors were unlikely to permit this final attrition. Galloway's bill of indictment accused the proprietor of maintaining a form of corruption no longer operative in England. Salkeld, he noted, had written that "no one ought to be Judge in his own Cause."[40] But the proprietor was accomplishing that end through the use of judicial tenure. "I can see little difference," Galloway concluded, "between a Person sitting Judge in his own Cause, and one who has Power to remove the Judge at Pleasure...."[41]

Galloway reiterated that secret proprietary instructions provided the most effective instrument of tyranny. The Assembly claimed the right to see proprietary instructions in much the same spirit Parliament addressed the king "for such Information as they judge necessary to their Deliberation...."[42] Penn used secret instructions to control funds to which he had never contributed, a right which, if acknowledged, would leave the Assembly without redress. Further, such power would place proprietor above king. Galloway pointed out that

> The King and Lords in Parliament...never, at present, presume to meddle with Supply Bills, or make amendments therein, and tho' Lords have heretofore attempted it, they were always obliged to give way, and have now left the Commons in the full Enjoyment of that essential Privilege of granting Supplies and Aids to the Crown, in their own way.[43]

It was Galloway's premise that good government demanded that the "private interest of the Ruler, co-operated with and [be] subservient to the Public Good." He also proclaimed his agreement with John Trenchard and Thomas Gordon that its opposite was "Unlimited Power...so wild and monstrous a Thing, that however it be to DESIRE it, it is as natural to OPPOSE it" nor ought it to be trusted with any mortal man, be his intentions ever so just: For besides that he will never CARE to part with it, he will rarely DARE." It was appropriate, then, that he should conclude with a plea to vacate the proprietary charter.[44]

In the five years that separated "Impartial State" from the official petition to the crown in 1764, Galloway's theory of politics remained unchanged. He believed that the proprietors deliberately undermined the guarantees of the constitution in order to augment their own powers; he believed that the most essential of popular rights, "the original right of Legislation," had been granted them by the crown and would be protected by the crown. Galloway contended that the only salvation lay in a change of charter which would grant "asylum from Slavery and Ruin."[45] The underlying concern he expressed here for the integrity of institutional power, whether in the Assembly, in Parliament, or in the crown, remained steadfast. In later years, when colonists challenged the power of Parliament, then the crown itself, he rejected his countrymen, as in 1764 he had rejected the proprietors.

Galloway said little in 1764 that he had not explained in

greater detail in 1759. The key to his thinking was his assumption that an equation could be made between English life at home and English life in the colonies. That identification once made, it was a short step to assume that the prerogatives obtained by the House of Commons were automatically transmitted to provincial assemblies in terms appropriate to the "nature of powers." In 1764, he also took the unique position that colonial legislation which had been approved by the crown was the equal of an act of Parliament and could not be repealed "by any Power, but that of the King, Lords, and Commons." Galloway, ironically, went so far as to approve the right of revolution to protect the Assembly's institutional integrity.[46] His description of king, ministers, and Parliament revealed his underlying attitudes: the king was all "Justice and benevolence," the ministers "Virtue and Morality," Parliament "the wisest Legislature in the World, renowned for their Justice in all Nations."[47] Galloway insisted that he would choose king, ministers, and Parliament over "this sink of Proprietary Injustice and ambition...."[48]

John Dickinson, unlike Galloway, opposed the change from proprietary to royal charter. Like Galloway, Dickinson took his stand for reasons which were to guide him through the next decade and beyond.

Dickinson's perspective was defined by a number of factors, and not the least important was the time spent in London exploring English politics. While in London Dickinson remarked at the close identity between the English constitution and English law.[49] He mused that London was a microcosm of the world, where "more is learned of mankind...in a month that can be in a year in any other part of the world."[50] Its diversity of rank, personalities, social graces, strengths and weaknesses made him marvel at the possibilities of newly-found maturity. "London takes off the rawness, and prejudices of youth & ignorance," he had advised his parents, having already assured them that he neither knew nor thought of the more illicit pleasures.[51]

Among life's vagaries, politicians seemed to intrigue Dickinson most. He had paid close attention to the machinations of Newcastle, the Earl of Holdernesse, Henry Pelham, and William Pitt, "a discontented statesman who is the patriot of the times & gives them [ministry] a good deal of trouble," noting with some dismay that the machinery of England's electoral processes were uniformly oiled by liquor or money.[52] Thomas Penn invited him to the King's birthday party. Dickinson emerged from the party with many hungers. The most immediate he soothed at a chophouse. But the other, for fame, some blue ribbons of his own, entrance to the small coteries rather than the large reception halls, required more delicate handling. In the end he made a more than rhetorical decision against the costs of fame. He could not bring himself to smile complacently for the favors of great men "at the expense of truth, reason &...country."[53] The most tentative gesture of subjugation could have no limitations. "When concessions are made to princes," he concluded, "tis as ridiculous to think of stopping as for a master of a ship to guess at the depth of water in an ebb tide....When its [power] has got a turn one way, there is no means in nature for altering its course but violence...English history will teach one this truth...so dangerous is what some people call complaisance & trust in their prince."[54]

What emerged from his political observations was a durable philosophical statement. The king could be seen with less personal cost from a distance: good (Whig) broadcloth did one as well as "a bit of ribbond." The world's amorphous standards were not to be his own when the results constantly showed "men sacrificing virtue, ease & reason...to gain those things to which mankind have falsely annexed confused ideas of what is desirable."[55]

The London experience did much to incline Dickinson toward his later directions. He sensed the strength and fragility of the political and constitutional structures. John Dickinson returned to Pennsylvania with a greater perception of the possible effect of human frailties upon the English constitution.

Dickinson also perceived that the colonial circumstance created opportunities for greater liberty in the colonies than in England. In his own colony, he argued, religious freedom, the absence of test oaths, and rotation of office, testified to beneficial conditions contrary to the English constitution and royal prerogatives. "Liberties!," he was to exclaim in his speech, were "founded on the acknowledge rights of human nature and restrained in our mother country, only by an unavoidable necessity of adhering in some measure to long-established custom."[56]

Dickinson's opposition to Pennsylvania's change of masters reflected his attitude toward legal processes. His struggle to conquer the intricacies of English common law had taught him of the law's slow and haphazard movement toward human liberty, and it taught him of the morass of precedent which made that liberty unexpectedly tenuous. He wrote of the law: "thus hath been formed between old errors and hasty innovations an entangled chain, that our ancestors either had not moderation or leisure enough to untwist."[57] The past, Dickinson concluded, spoke not of a human liberty guaranteed since time immemorial, but instead made silent testimony to the frailty of liberty and the ease with which it is lost.

Dickinson's perspectives led him to oppose the vast majority in the Assembly who favored turning to royal power. William Smith wrote the preface to Dickinson's published statement, and in that preface he hit upon its major theme, the transfer would deprive the colony of known and advantageous rights without guaranteeing any in return.[58] Dickinson pointed out that the Assembly's assumptions of royal good faith stood on nebulous grounds. For example, the crown had not interfered to oppose the proprietary tax exemption, but instead the king had viewed the colonial protests "to be illegal attempts, and pernicious pretensions."[59] He feared that the cure ("a blaze of royal authority") would prove more oppressive than the illness (untaxed proprietors.)[60]

The same hesitancy that prevented Dickinson from joining his fellows in supporting the royal petition later robbed him of a place in the pantheon of independence. Dickinson had a great preoccupation with the problem of faulty timing, and he had collected a bag full of historical disasters to prove the dangers therein. From Rapin's History of England, he pulled the untimely performance of the Duke of Monmouth which had led to the (fortunate) success of William of Orange.[61] He turned, also, to the.enormously popular An Account of Denmark as it was in the Year 1692, by Robert Molesworth, one of the commonwealthmen described by Caroline Robbins as "the most widely quoted and probably the most influential among the liberal Whigs, in his lifetime and for a considerable time thereafter."[62]

Molesworth wrote his book after an unhappy diplomatic experience in Denmark. He had been sent on a private mission in 1689. In 1692, he went again as envoy extraordinary. However, molesworth soon offended the king, and he was forced to leave unceremoniously for poaching on the king's private reserves and forcing passage of a road exclusively reserved for the royal chariots."[63] In response to his unheralded exit, Molesworth wrote An Account of Denmark..., describing the government as arbitrary and an object lesson for all to see. This book, partially in support of revolution, and partially anti-clerical, gained popularity and distinction for Molesworth.

The theme of his book was the blessing of liberty and the ease with which it could be lost. "Health and Liberty are, without dispute," he wrote, "the greatest natural Blessings Mankind is capable of enjoying; I say natural, because the contrary States are purely accidental, and arise from Nature debauched, depraved or enforced."[64] By describing the dangers to which a constitution is subject, he hoped to avoid the necessity of actual experience. He admonished that, "'Tis a great, yet rare Advantage to learn rightly how to prize HEALTH without the Expence of being sick; but one may easily and cheaply grow sensible of the true value of LIBERTY, by travelling into such Countries, for a Season, as do not enjoy it."[65] Denmark, for Molesworth, was an example of monarchy turned tyranny, and of people, once watchful, now indolent. The moral was obvious: here is a people, once free, who have let their liberties be taken from them. See how it was done, how they repent; we should take heed. For Dickinson, the lesson was a real one. The Danish commons, he wrote, making an obvious comparison with Pennsylvania, "smarting under the tyranny of their nobility, in n fit of revengeful fury _suddenly_ surrendered their liberties to their _king;_ and ever since, with unavailing brief and useless execrations, have detested the _mad moment_ which slipt upon them tho shackles of slavery, which no struggles can shake off."[66]

Dickinson then turned to the _Annals_ of Tacitus for the final example, that of men ruined by ambition and haste, "which misfortune hath happened to many good men, who despising those things which they might slowly and safely attain, seize them too hastily, and with fatal speed rush upon their own destruction."[67]

Dickinson avoided the question of proper timing for a new charter by making ambiguous suggestions about a period when the proprietors no longer had male heirs or, for other reasons, happily transferred control.[68] But he made astute observations about the political state of England. For one, the king had been displeased with Pennsylvania's conduct during the recent war and his anger had mounted over their constitutional debates. Second, he pointed out that the king and his ministers were political creatures. Obviously, the crown and proprietors shared an identity of interest, "The tale of ministerial favour has in all seasons blown propitious to proprietary interests, why," he asked, "do we now fondly flatter ourselves that it will suddenly shift its quarter..?"[69] Dickinson insisted that a petition to the crown would encourage English politicians in their natural pursuit of power. Once "the affair is laid before Parliament, the desires of the ministry are insinuated, the rights of the Crown are vindicated, and an act passes to deliver us at once from the government of Proprietors, and the privileges we claim under them."[70] His conclusion brought no surprise: "Power," he said, "is like an ocean, not easily admitting limits to be fixed in it." Their privileges were so closely tied to the proprietary charter, that to divorce the two would endanger both. Why not, he suggested, merely obtain a royal opinion on issues of colonial prerogative before making the fateful leap?[71]

As Galloway gleefully remarked, Dickinson's speech changed few votes. It took the end of the French and Indian War, with the new imperial policy that followed' to prick that particular balloon.

What had taken place in Pennsylvania during the constitutional turmoil had significance for the imperial crisis to follow. The Assembly's battle with proprietary privilege forced them to consider the question of Pennsylvania's relationship to the whole of the empire. The proprietor's role complicated the issue, but the colonists reached conclusions which bore the scrutiny of the coming decade: Englishmen in America were the political equals of Englishmen at home. To that end they claimed for the Assembly the full powers of a representative legislature and denied to the proprietor rights he claimed to issue secret and binding restraints over legislation and to control internal taxation. It soon became apparent that the proprietor's claims in Pennsylvania were not unique, that, instead, they had foreshadowed imperial policy in which Parliament, not an Englishman, made claims to supremacy. That challenge became the issue of the moment.

Footnotes

[1] The Pennsylvania constitution of 1776 was divided into three sections, the Preamble, the Declaration of Rights, and the Frame of Government The Preamble advocated staples of whig theory, the social compact, the "natural rights" of men, popular sovereignty and the right of revolution. The Declaration of Rights guaranteed freedom of speech and religious liberty for those who believed in the Old and New Testament. The Frame of Government created most dissension. For example, is granted exclusive rights to a unicameral legislature. In addition, there was an executive council, but it had no veto power" the Council of Censors only initiated amendments. Of interest were the social changes indicative of the dissident forces now in control: the Frame abolished property qualifications for voting and imprisonment for debt. Voting and office-holding required an oath of allegiance to the constitution and government. See J. Paul Selsam, Pennsylvania Constitution of 1776: A Study in Revolutionary Democracy (Phil., 1936), 176-204.

[2] The tale of William Penn in the colonies is a familiar one. From the perspective of intellectual influence it is only important to note that Penn inculcated a variety of whiggish principles which his colonists took seriously but which he was incapable of fulfilling. The early history of the colony was full of bickering between the settlers and Penn over their political and economic rights. The charter of 1701 marked the colonists' victory in their

battle for full Assembly prerogatives. See Mary Maples Dunn, William Penn' Politics and Conscience (Princeton, 1967), passim: J. R. Pole, Political Representation in England and the Origins of the American Republic (London, New York, 1966), passim: Gary B. Nash, "The Framing of Government in Pennsylvania, Ideas in Contrast with Reality," WMQ, 3d Ser., XXVI (1969), 578-85: H. F. Russell Smith, Harrington and his Oceana, A Study of A Seventeenth Century Utopia and its Influence in America (Cambridge, 1914), 18, 143-46, 178-89.

[3] See a petition signed by Franklin and others warning the proprietors that they stood in danger of losing "the Affections of their People, a loss, which...will be found of more consequence to them than they seem at present to be aware of." Pennsylvania Archives, 8 Ser., V, 3827.

[4] Lawrence Henry Gipson, The British Empire Before the American Revolution (New York, 1960), III, 158, 161-62.

[5] G. B. Warden, "The Proprietary Group in Pennsylvania, 1754-1764," MWQ, 3d Ser., XXI (1964), 369-84.

[6] Samuel Hazard, Annals of Pennsylvania...1609-1682 (Philadelphia, 1850), 502.

[7] Quoted in Frederick B. Tolles, Meeting House and Counting House: The Quaker Merchants of Colonial Philadelphia, 1682-1783 (New York, 1963), 25.

[8] Pennsylvania Archives, 8 Ser., VI, 4391-92.

[9] Dr. John Fothergill, the London Quaker patriarch, reported

to his Pennsylvania counterpart, Israel Pemberton, that John Carteret, the second Earl Granville, had "advised that we should use our utmost endeavors to prevail upon Friends in Pennsylvania, not to accept seats in the house at this juncture...otherwise they would be totally incapacitated for ever." See Theodore Thayer, Israel Pemberton. King of the Quakers (Philadelphia, 1943), 115-16: Pennsylvania Archives. 1 Ser., VII, 292, 148-49! ibid., 8 Ser., VI, 4385. The four Quakers who resigned after re-election cited ministerial request as their reason.

[10] Franklin to Peter Collinson, November 5, 1756, Leonard W. Labaree, ed., The Papers of Benjamin Franklin (New Haven, 1959), VII, 9-10 (hereafter cited as Franklin Papers.)

[11] Pennsylvania Archives, 1 Ser., VI, 600. Morris had written that Franklin "is at the head of these extraordinary measures taken by the Assembly, writes their messages and directs their motions."

[12] See James H. Hutson, "Benjamin Franklin and Pennsylvania Politics, 1751-1755: A Reappraisal," PMHB, XCIII (1969), 303-04. He cites William S. Hanna, Norman J. Cohen, and Gary B. Nash as historians who treat Pennsylvania politics as a fight over power devoid of principle. Hutson rejects the "unprinciples" interpretation and argues that "Rather, it appears that in so far as Franklin reflects the nature of the political process in the province, the venerable whig theory... insistence on the primacy of principle in political affairs...,provides the most accurate conceptual framework for explaining Pennsylvania politics during

these years." Also see ibid., 310-11, 317, 353.

[13] Sister Joan de Lourdes Leonard, C.S.J., "Elections in Colonial Pennsylvania," WMQ, 3d Ser., XI (1954), 385-86, 387n. Benjamin Chew also noted this phenomenon in 1764 after the election of Dickinson and other Quakers. "The measures and plan of each day's proceedings (was) being settled by them [candidates] every evening at private meetings & cabals had with their Friends in the house." Penn Official Correspondence, IX, 286. Quoted in Raymond Clarence Werner, "Joseph Galloway' His Life and Times" "unpubl. Ph.D. diss., University of Iowa, 1927), 75-76. Franklin remarked that his newspaper had brought him proprietary attention' "leading Men, seeing a News Paper now in the hands of one who could also handle a Pen, thought it convenient to oblige and encourage me." See Benjamin Franklin, Autobiography. ed. Leonard W. Labaree (New Haven and London, 1964), 121.

[14] Pennsylvania Archives. 8 Ser., VI, 4383. The election returns showed Galloway, Isaac Norris, Joseph Fox, Thomas Leech, and John Hughes elected from Philadelphia County, Franklin and William McMaster from Philadelphia, and William Allen from Northampton. Norris was elected Speaker. Galloway's biographer, Ernest Baldwin, remarked, "It became necessary to send men Cow the Assembly who would not scruple to vote suitable military protection, and at the same time would serve the interests of the Quaker party and its German followers." See Ernest H. Baldwin, Joseph Galloway' The Loyalist Politician (Philadelphia, 1902), 12.

[15] Quoted in David L. Jacobson, "John Dickinson and Joseph Galloway, 1764-1776: A Study in Contrasts" (unpubl. Ph.D. diss., Princeton University, 1959), 14.

[16] Pennsylvania Archives, 8 Ser., VI. 4557, 4562. Galloway replaced Franklin on the Committee of Aggrievances, the Committee of Correspondence, and the Committee for revising and correcting Minutes: Franklin Cow Galloway, April 11, 1758, Franklin Papers, VII,. 179.

[17] Pennsylvania Archives, 8 Ser., VI, 4505, 4520.

[18] Ibid., 4537-42.

[19] Ibid., 4925-26.

[20] Isaac Norris to Franklin, April 4, 1757, Franklin Papers, VII, 171.

[21] Franklin wrote to Isaac Norris of Penn's claims, then added "and That [statement of prerogatives] He said with a Kind of triumphing Insolence, such as a low Jockey might do when a Purchaser complained that He had cheated him in a Horse. I...conceived that moment a more cordial and thorough Contempt for him than I ever felt for any Man living...," Jan. 14, 1758, ibid., 361-62; Franklin's interview with John Carteret, Lord Granville (he was married to Thomas Penn's sister-in-law), revealed the close philosophical ties between proprietor and Crown. Granville told Franklin, "you Americans have wrong Ideas about the Nature of your Constitution: you contend that the King's Instructions to his Governors are not Laws, and think yourselves at Liberty to

disregard them at your own Discretion....They are so far as relates Cow you, the Law of the Land: for THE KING IS THE LEGISLATOR OF THE COLONIES." Franklin responded, "I had always understood from our Charters, that our Laws were to be made by our Assemblies to be presented indeed to the King for his Royal Assent, but that once given the King could not repeal or alter them. And as the Assemblies could not make permanent Laws without his Assent, so neither could he make a Law for them without theirs." That Granville disagreed made Franklin momentarily pause' "his Lordship's Conversation...a little alarmed me as to what might be the sentiments of the Court concerning us...," Aug. 20, 1757, ibid., VII, 248-51.

[22] Quoted in John H. Powell, "John Dickinson: Penman of the Revolution." (unpubl. Ph.D. diss., University of Iowa, 1938), 148.

[23] Stille reports that Dickinson and Galloway opposed Moland and Chew before the Supreme Court in April term, 1760, and he finds this suggestive of their high stature. See Charles Stille, Life and Times of John Dickinson, 1732-1802 (Philadelphia, 1891), 36-37. For Dickinson's election and committee assignments, see Pennsylvania Archives, 8 Ser., VI, 5367, 5383, 5476.

[24] Joseph Galloway, A True and Impartial State of the Province of Pennsylvania (Philadelphia, 1759). (Historical Society of Pennsylvania).

[25] William Smith, A Brief State of the Province of Pennsylvania (London, 1755).

[26] Ibid., 9.

[27] Ibid., 10-11.

[28] Galloway, Impartial State, 22.

[29] Ibid., "Dedication."

[30] Ibid., 24-25.

[31] Ibid., 25.

[32] Ibid., 10. Montesquieu wrote" "A character so extraordinary in the institutions of Greece, has shewn itself lately in the dregs and corruption of modern times. A very honest legislator has formed a peoples, to whom probity seems as natural as bravery Cow the Spartans. Mr. Penn is a real Lycurgus...they resemble one another in the ascendant they had over free men, in the prejudices they overcame, and in the passion which they Subdues." Spirit of the Laws, trans. Thomas Nugent (London, 1773), Book IV, ch. 6.

[33] Galloway, Impartial State, iii.

[34] Ibid., 26-28.

[35] Ibid., 28.

[36] Ibid., 30. Galloway's claim that proprietary instructions violated their charters and English laws was based on "the Nature of Powers. which the Law has been careful to keep entire. as the only means to preserve good Order in Governments established under the English Constitution, where no such Absurdity and Ihconvenience was ever allowed of, as to give the Persons represented, a Power to control their Representatives...."

[37] Ibid.,6, 13-15.

[38] Ibid., 36.

[39] Ibid., 55-56.

40 Ibid., 34; William Salkeld, Reports of the Cases in the King's Bench, 1689-1712 (London, 17117-18): Bernard Knollenberg, Origin of the American Revolution. 1759-1766 (New York, 1960), 71-74: In 1760, Galloway expanded on his judicial views in a pamphlet, "A Letter to the People of Pennsylvania; Occasioned by the Assembly's Passing that Important Act, for Constituting the Judges of the Supreme Courts and Common Pleas, During Good Behaviour," in Bernard Bailyn, ed, Pamphlets of the American Revolution. 1750-1776 (Cambridge, 1965), 257-72,
249-52. Considering judicial quality, impermanence seems to have had advantages.

[41] Galloway, Impartial State, 34.

[42] Ibid., 96.

[43] Ibid., 80.

[44] Ibid., 21-22. See Thomas Gordon and John Trenchard, Cato's Letters (#115). The most readily available edition is that edited by David C. Jacobson, The English Libertarian Heritage...(New York, 1965), 256-60.

[45] Galloway, Impartial State, 172-73.

[46] Galloway, Speech...to...John Dickinson (Phil., 1764), 4-[47]
Ibid., 8, 24.

[48] Ibid., 10.

[49] Dickinson, London Letters, 450.

[50] Ibid., 269.

[51] Ibid., 262.

[52] Ibid., 266, 443.

[53] Ibid., 445.

[54] Ibid., 449.

[55] Ibid., 430-31.

[56] Dickinson, "A Speech on a Petition for a Change of Government of the Colony of Pennsylvania, May 24, 1764, with a preface by Rev. William Smith," Paul Leicester Ford., The Writings of John Dickinson (Philadelphia, 1895), 34-35 (hereafter cited as Dickinson, Speech...May 1764).

[57] Ibid., 34.

[58] William Smith, "Preface," to Dickinson, Speech... May, 1764, 18. He wrote, "our representatives, by their present petition, seem...to have offered up our whole charter rights, leaving it to the grace of others to return us any part, or indeed no part of them, according as it may be thought proper."

[59] Dickinson, Speech...May 1764, 21-22.

[60] Ibid., 21-23.

[61] Paul Rapin-Thoyras, The History of England, trans. by N. Tindal (London, 1723), III, 746-49.

[62] Robbins, Commonwealthman, 91.

[63] DNB.

[64] Robert Molesworth, An Account of Denmark as it was in the Year 1692 (London, 1738), Preface.

[66] Dickinson, *Speech...May 1764*, 23-24.

[67] *Ibid*: *Annals*, Book III, no. 66.

[68] Dickinson, *Speech...May 1764*, 27.

[69] *Ibid*., 23.

[70] *Ibid*., 31.

[71] *Ibid*., 34-34.

CHAPTER FOUR

THE FIRST STAGE, 1765 to 1770

The demands for revenue made by Grenville and Townshend in the name of parliamentary supremacy forced colonists to reconsider the legitimacy of that supremacy and the function of sovereignty within the British empire. In the years from 1764 to 1770 colonial lawyers became convinced that the constitutional settlement which resulted from the Glorious Revolution had neglected the problems of empire. They questioned the pertinence of English common law to the colonies. They debated whether a literal interpretation of the English constitution guaranteed them equal rights and privileges. Many lawyers, Galloway for one, committed themselves to the principles of 1689 -- a limited monarchy, parliamentary supremacy, and separation of powers. Other lawyers, among whom were Dickinson and Wilson, paraphrased English legal traditions so that by redefining procedures the spirit of balance of power and representative government might be preserved. The first stage, that of redefinition, took place during the Grenville-Townshend period; the second stage, the application of principle to politics, led to the Revolution. The first stage is the subject of this chapter.

The colonists increasingly identified their cause with the

English struggle against tyranny a century earlier. They argued that the Glorious Revolution had substituted parliamentary supremacy for royal supremacy, but, thereafter, Parliament had claimed unlimited supremacy as well. Many insisted on the need to rebalance the government in favor of the crown and provincial assemblies in order to preserve the mixed constitution of 1689. On a large scale the issues in eighteenth-century America seemed to differ little from those in seventeenth-century England: return to the ancient constitution, limitations upon unlimited prerogative, and political representation for those with a stake in society.

By 1770 John Dickinson had helped remold colonial constitutional concepts. From his pen had come the resolutions of the Pennsylvania Assembly and of the Stamp Act Congress which rejected Parliament's claim to taxing power. In the wake of the Townshend program Dickinson wrote the "Letters from a Farmer in Pennsylvania," which attacked all imperial taxation on constitutional grounds. He had earlier revealed elements of his perspective during Pennsylvania's charter crisis. His skepticism of royal and ministerial integrity had led him to support separation of colonial and English interests. Further, he had shown a sense of the large role played by custom and usage in the haphazard development of English common law. Dickinson turned to such stalwarts as Edward Coke for a vision of the ancient constitution and to David Hume, a contemporary who combined the staples of the common law mind with a refreshing vision of change and adaptability in the law. The result was Dickinson's early and radical view of parliamentary limitations which redefined seventeenth-century principles in eighteenth-century terms.

In contrast to Dickinson, Joseph Galloway made but tentative gestures of protest against taxation. More important to him than aversion to the Stamp Act was his commitment to the settlement of 1689 and the parliamentary supremacy supported by Burlamaqui and Blackstone. In the name of "Americanus" he published proposals designed to preserve the authority of Parliament, with or without the stamp tax. From 1764 to 1774, Galloway controlled the Pennsylvania Assembly as its speaker, and during that time he devoted his influence to warding off the chaos he envisioned in the wake of constitutional collapse. Galloway, too, had earlier revealed his basic principles. He trusted the king and his ministers. He identified constitutional stability with the Glorious Revolution, and he accepted in literal form the entire body of English law and applied it to the colonial scene. Parliamentary supremacy provided a voice for the propertied classes and fulfilled the need for indivisible sovereignty within the empire. He found authoritative confirmation for the essential role of legislative supremacy and, thus armed, took his first steps toward political obsolescence.

The Stamp Act and the Townshend duties forced Dickinson and Galloway to take the measure of their constitutional theories.

Dickinson's broad perspective parted from Galloway's literal interpretation as it had in the charter crisis and made opponents of them in the coming imperial strife.

i

Joseph Galloway opposed the Stamp Act: but because he did little explanatory writing until his political career ended in exile, there are only fragments of information in letters to Franklin and in the proposals by "Americanus" for ending the Stamp Act crisis. All of these underlined Galloway's constant concern for the institutional integrity of the Parliament of Great Britain and for the constitutional structure which it represented.

In August, 1765, an article by "Americanus" appeared in the Pennsylvania Journal. Galloway advised Franklin that he had written it as "a moderate Piece" designed to quell the "many Outrages and Riots" which had greeted the Stamp Act.[1] In the article, Galloway accepted the colonists' obligation to contribute to the British treasury and, simultaneously, dismissed the feasibility of the requisition system. Who, then, he asked, should enforce the contributions? Left to a choice between Parliament and the colonial assemblies Galloway endorsed the claims of the assemblies.[2] He proposed two alternative means by which the colonists could ensure taxation through their own consent. First, since cooperation among independent colonial assemblies was impossible, he suggested "an united legislature of the colonies, free from the objections arising from the present state of our distinct and several legislatures...."[3] Second, he suggested petitioning for representation in Parliament as a possible alternative to a single colonial legislature. Either alternative, he wrote, would eliminate "imposition of taxes without our consent...."[4]

Galloway gave Franklin more substantive information about his proposals. He praised the plan for providing greater ease of communication within the empire and for quieting the mounting opposition to Parliament. Throughout, Galloway reiterated his concern for imperial welfare epitomized by parliamentary sovereignty. He wrote of his plan: "It can no way Affect, but rather promote the Interest of the Mother Country, as a new door of Information,...will be opened....I am convinced it will remove all uneasiness and restore the Colonies to her former Obedience."[5] Later, he wrote of his horror at the thought of rebellion. He believed firmly, he told Franklin, that if the colonies were represented.within the empire according to the proposals he had fashioned, they would then be enticed back to the bonds of union. Prudence dictated that the colonies and England be united by whatever "Measure that can be devised."[6] With that in mind, "Americanus" endorsed the proposal for a Stamp Act Congress, both as a first step toward a colonial legislature and as a means of limiting the grounds for violence.[7] The results did not meet

Galloway's expectations. The resolutions of the Congress, drafted by John Dickinson, went beyond his hoped-for moderation.[8] The only feasible solution, he concluded, was to repeal the act.[9]

Galloway's political operations in the Assembly left him little time for activity other than letter writing. In 1783, when he lived in England in exile, Galloway wrote an essay which clarified his attitudes during the pre-revolutionary period, although it was without the compromise he had hoped for in 1765. In _Political Reflections on the Late Colonial Governments_, Galloway outlined his constitutional philosophy, laid bare his sources, and revealed his vision of the British empire. One would expect Galloway to rely on Blackstone, whose concept of imperial sovereignty made him first famous and then infamous to the colonists. Instead, he turned to Blackstone's predecessor, the Genevan political scientist and teacher, Jean Jacques Burlamaqui, whose influence stretched from Blackstone and Galloway to James Otis, James Wilson, and Thomas Jefferson. Burlamaqui's _The Principles of Natural and Political Law_ (1747) was used in Cambridge, Oxford, and Dublin, in President Witherspoon's Princeton, and in William and Mary after 1749. Quantitatively, Burlamaqui enjoyed greater popularity than did Locke, although revolutionary lore has ignored his influence.[10] Burlamaqui's two volumes, one on natural law, the other on political law, concerned themselves with two aspects of the same problem: the ends of government and the political structures necessary to attain those ends. Governments had been instituted, he wrote, to attain the collective happiness of the constituent parts, and law (which he defined as the relationship between these parts) provided the instruments for that goal. Two themes are essential to an understanding of Galloway's sympathetic response: Burlamaqui insisted on the necessity of happiness within the social and political structure, happiness which emerged from proper relationships depended upon the acceptance of sovereignty. This, in turn, implied recognition of superiors and inferiors within society.

The proper relationship between superiors and inferiors provided the cement of society and the means to social happiness. The people were the source of sovereignty, but they had transferred their power to a superior whose honor, wisdom, and goodness they recognized as greater than their own. Thus a subject was able "to pursue his real interest, and to choose the surest and best way to attain the end he is designed for, which is happiness."[11] Subjects, as Burlamaqui defined them, were intrinsically "persons, that are under the obligation of obeying."[12] Because both subjects and sovereign were defined by their function, the happiness of each was determined by the extent to which they fulfilled their identities: a happy monarch was one who used his honor, wisdom, and goodness for his subjects; happy subjects gloried in their trust in the superior to whom they had granted sovereignty and whom they obeyed. That relationship Burlamaqui described as "the Right we call Law."[13]

The right to command must be based on reason, but reason

(directed toward happiness) enforced obedience. Burlamaqui assured his readers that "this will of the superior has nothing in it contrary to reason....In order to render a law the rule of human actions, it should be absolutely agreeable to the nature and constitution of man, and be ultimately designed for his happiness. which reason makes him necessarily pursue."[14] Burlamaqui made one further logical extension of his identification of object and function; he proposed that an institution, by its very nature, cannot give away any part of its powers, a premise which Galloway voiced in 1759 during debates over the Pennsylvania charter. It was with this emphasis on a political definition of happiness and society's intrinsic need for indivisible sovereignty that Galloway wrote his Political Reflections.

Civil society, Galloway wrote in terms highly reminiscent of Burlamaqui, was a political system originally formed by individuals who had granted their power to a sovereign in exchange for security. The premises of that society rested on a supreme authority which dictated "regulation and final decision of every matter susceptible of human direction, which relates to the safety and happiness of society."[15] The superior-inferior relationship was essential, but each form of government -- monarchy, aristocracy, or democracy had an intrinsic structure which uniquely embellished the basic principle of sovereignty. Galloway defined the proper operations of an institution, as did Burlamaqui, by its function or by the "nature of powers," to use Galloway's earlier phrase.

He wrote, "The genius and character, the fundamental laws and principles, of that particular form we mean to establish, must always be regarded in the construction; and if we mean to preserve it, care must be taken that no heterogeneous ingredients or principles be admitted, because they must tend to change its nature, and in the end to destroy it."[16]

The British constitution, with which Galloway was primarily concerned, had managed a harmonious balance among the different forms, thereby mitigating against "the mischiefs which are naturally produced by each system in its separate state."[17] But that happiness which Galloway defined as the product of the British constitution was a Burlamaquian public happiness, and those who opposed it had preferred "their own private views."[18] The preservation of that public good which Galloway cherished depended upon "a strict attention and adherence to those original laws and principles by which it was formed. Every deviation from them, every change in the structure of its parts and members, every introduction of heterogeneous matter, must produce disorder and confusion.[19] To introduce republicanism into a mixed monarchy would have that result.

The British constitution, of course, belonged to a mixed form of government.[20] The monarch had several functions. He held the supreme executive authority as well as primacy in the supreme legislative authority held by king, lords, and commons. The monarch's task was to "superintend" .the execution and preservation of the laws and fundamental principles, but neither the executive nor the legislative had the power to change or destroy the constitution, only to preserve it.

The role of fundamental laws in preserving the unique qualities of the British constitution had been described by Burlamaqui, whom Galloway lauded for being "concise and perspicacious."[21] The Genevan had defined fundamental laws as the decrees by which a people decided upon a particular form of government, but also as the entire covenant system between the superior and inferior members Galloway endorsed designed to limit sovereignty.[22] Galloway endorse Burlamaqui's supposition that fundamental law obliged a sovereign to use his power "agreeably to the <u>general rule of the public good</u>."[23] In defining an institution according to its function and fundamental law, it was a logical (if naive) step to conclude that in a limited monarchy' "It is a happy incapacity in Kings, <u>not to be able to act contrary to the laws of the land</u>."[24] The common law modified traditions and statutes, thereby providing guidelines for society.[25]

Galloway established certain basic premises: society depended upon sovereignty, the extent of which was defined by the inherent functions of mixed monarchy and the restrictions of fundamental law; no institution could act contrary to its nature or function, or in any way which would lead to the destruction rather than the enhancement of the entire society. Within that framework, Galloway turned his attention to imperial relations or, to use his term, the creation of inferior societies.

Galloway located the power to create inferior corporations in the category of ill-defined royal prerogatives, limited by the "original decrees and fundamental laws of the British Government."[26] By which he meant that the creation of inferior corporations must comply with the principle of strengthening and preserving the British constitution. Pufendorf, Montesquieu, Vattel, and Burlamaqui all reinforced Galloway's assertion that any action contrary to the strength and preservation of the British constitution must be null and void.[27] Therefore. the creation of an equal corporation would be unconstitutional. Citing Pufendorf, Galloway asserted:

> if there could be a body of men not subject to THE regulation of the CIVIL Government, there would be a State within a State...for if he (Monarch) hath given or ascertained to them, in express words, an absolute independent right with regard even to some particular affairs then he hath plainly abdicated his authority, and, by admitting two heads in the constitution, hath rendered it irregular and MONSTROUS.[28]

Galloway added that the most important prerogative which a monarch could not, in the nature of things, give away was the power of taxation "upon which the defense and safety of every part of the empire materially and essentially depend."[29] Galloway perceived the king's functions to include the right to create inferior bodies whose structure duplicated the principles of mixed government; prerogative did not include the right to create corporations equal to the British state which would destroy the "order, unity, and spirit of the Government." The king could not change the fundamental constitution of the land, he could not alienate the rights of Lords or Commons, and in the same spirit, he could not create inferior communities independent of the state. Nor could the king exempt inferior bodies from the law of the land -- the common law ("ancient usage and immemorial consent") or statutory law. It was significant to Galloway that the English constitution expressed these restrictions as "the king shall not." Galloway contended that the spirit of limited monarchy, the essence of 1688, depended upon that essential restriction. "If the Crown may deviate in any degree from the original polity and fundamental laws of the principle society in the establishment of its subordinate members, there are no other lines by which it may be restrained."[30]

Having invoked the ancient constitution, Galloway turned to the problem of inferior corporations in America. The land had been "annexed to the kingdom of England" and thus became subject to its government and the royal prerogative. Because of political necessity, the crown and Parliament had granted the colonists "certain limited powers and rights...,subject always to the control of the supreme Legislature." The limitations, he added, had been defined in the British constitution.[31]

Galloway charged that from the beginning the colonial charters with their "over-prevalent principles of democracy," had eaten away at the institutional harmony of the British empire.[32]

They had done so by rejecting the essential concept of a supreme authority and the obedience due that authority. Britain's been threatened. Galloway spoke to Americans and Englishmen alike when he warned: "Should these relations between the sovereign power and the subordinate member be universally dissolved, the society is no more; should they partially, or in regard to a part of the members, be broken, the strength of the society must be diminished in proportion."[33] The strength of the whole stemmed from the mutual dependence of all the elements because, Galloway observed, "their dependence on the supreme authority for what relates to their safety and happiness constitutes their membership, and unites them with the society."[34]

Galloway had accepted Burlamaqui's concept of a public happiness generated and protected by a superior power. The relationship of superiors and inferiors Galloway regarded as essential to the public good. In the mixed constitution of Great Britain Parliament had become sovereign; therefore the colonies must take an inferior role. Burlamaqui had also defined institutions through their functions. Galloway pursued that concept as "the nature of powers." He argued constantly for the purity of institutions: "republicanism" would destroy the delicate balance of mixed government; so, too, would an enhanced role for provincial legislatures in violation of parliamentary sovereignty.

The American charters had unbalanced that delicate and fragile relationship. They had neglected dependency upon Parliament; in fact, the colonists had insisted upon a monstrous equality in violation of the essence of the British constitution. Without due subordination and without enforcement, the inevitable results were rebellion, revolt, and independence for the colonies and, Galloway feared, national insignificance for Great Britain.[35] In 1774 Galloway would make his plea for reform within the British empire in order to avoid these dire consequences.

ii

John Dickinson spent the years 1764 to 1770 leading his countrymen away form the constitutional views supported by Joseph Galloway. In the years between the Stamp Act and the Townshend duties, Dickinson authored many important public statements: the resolves passed by the Pennsylvania Assembly (1765), the resolutions adopted by the Stamp Act Congress (1765), and the Petition to the King (1765). In his own name, he wrote "Address to Friends and Countrymen, November 1765," a pamphlet on "The Late Regulations Respecting the British Colonies Considered, December 1765," " A Letter to the Committee of Correspondence in Barbados," written at the end of the first crisis, and, of course, the famous _Letters from A Farmer in Pennsylvania_. With increasing sophistication, Dickinson played on two major themes, (1) the advantages of the pre-1763 mercantile relationship to Great Britain, and (2) the rights to liberty and happiness enjoyed by the colonists in exchange.

Dickinson's initial responses to the Stamp Act in the Pennsylvania Assembly and in the Stamp Act Congress were essentially dress-rehearsals for his later arguments. In his draft for the Pennsylvania resolves, for example, Dickinson argued that the colony's constitutional guarantees rested on "the natural Rights of Mankind, and on the noble Principles of English Liberty...."[36] The stamp duties violated the constitution by depriving colonists of taxation only by popular consent. "Consent" depended on two criteria. The power to tax belonged to the crown or its representatives and, "for the Time being," to the local assembly.[37] Dickinson also claimed that custom and usage had evolved so that the local legislature possessed "exclusive Right of levying Taxes upon Themselves."[38] He concluded with a warning that unless the British repealed the Stamp Act, the mother country would be threatened with economic disaster.

A number of popular misconceptions appeared in Dickinson's first statement. For example, Dickinson alternately used the terms "internal taxes" and "taxes" in his draft of protest, although the assembly's official statement was unambiguously opposed to "taxes."[39] Also, Dickinson, unlike the Assembly, left the door open for colonial representation in Parliament when he spoke of the assembly's authority "for the time being." He added, however, that custom and usage had empowered only the provincial legislatures.

Dickinson's draft for the Stamp Act Congress proved more precise. In it, the colonies recognized the authority of the crown and the right of Parliament to legislate in areas "not inconsistent with the principles of freedom." More precisely, Dickinson claimed that taxation by assemblies provided the only insurance for popular consent. In a sense, much of the emphasis of the next decade on fundamental law was previewed here by Dickinson. It was in the name of the principles of the British constitution that Dickinson made his claim for colonial legislatures. If, as Coke had written, only commons had the right to make grants, and if these grants were indeed gifts from the people to the crown, as Dickinson agreed they were, then it was inconsistent with the spirit of that tradition for commons to grant the king not their own property but "the property of the colonists."[40]

Dickinson's later statements on the Stamp Act only refined his initial reverence for Coke's interpretation of Magna Carta and its confirmation of 1688. It was in Coke's terms that he wrote the Petition to the King stressing the colonists' rights to trial by jury under common law procedures and to local control of taxation.[41] It was also in Coke's terms that he proposed, in 1766, "the immutable maxims of reason and justice," as grounds not only for the Glorious Revolution but for the equally glorious stand against the Stamp Act.[42]

The threat of unfavorable discrimination developed into an important theme in Dickinson's writings. Rights not only implied security of property, but also equality. In his "Address to Friends and Countrymen," he warned: "Rouse yourselves, think, oh! think of the endless Miseries you _must_ entail upon yourselves and your Country, by touching the pestilential Cargoes [stamps] that have been sent you."[43] Their choice, he wrote, lay between freedom and slavery. Freedom demanded security of property. If the colonists permitted Parliament to create a successful precedent they would become for the British "Hewers of wood, and Drawers of Water." They must consider the Stamp Act a test case of British power which would grow stronger with use. "Power," Dickinson advised, "is of a tenacious Nature, What it seizes, it will retain." [44] Their salvation lay in treating the problem with disdain and proceeding "in all Business as usual."[45] In that same theme Dickinson wrote to William Pitt in December 1765, to encourage repeal of the Stamp Act. In words which he himself forgot by 1776, Dickinson warned Pitt that in the right circumstances the colonists could successfully revolt with European aid.[46] If the colonists ever became convinced that the British pursued a deliberate policy of subordination -- restrictions upon colonial trade, further extensions of prerogative in the colonies, and taxation without their consent -- revolution would follow. He wrote:

> The Mother Country cannot be too tender in taking from the Colonies such Privileges [sic] or immunities which she herself enjoys. Such treatment must produce odious and inflaming Comparisons; and while they think themselves, as they will always think themselves, entitled to the same Rights with hers, they will esteem those Restrictions, insulting Abuses of her Power, and Their condition as a state of Slavery. From this...they will endeavor to escape -- But this may not be, till these Restrictions are generally felt. [47]

That same month Dickinson reiterated the danger of unequal treatment in his pamphlet, "The Late Regulations Respecting the British Colonies Considered."[48] He took as his theme Montesquieu's definition of slavery: "renouncing the use of those things which nature has given them: or in being OBLIGED TO SUBMIT TO A DISADVANTAGEOUS COMMERCE."[49] What followed was a litany of discrimination: the Sugar Act, the Currency Act, taxation without colonial consent, attacks on colonial legislative power, a standing army in peacetime, and violations of the right to trial by jury.[50] The lesson to be learned, Dickinson concluded, was the growing distinction between the interests of the British empire and the interests of British North America.[51]

The list grew longer: although Parliament repealed the Stamp Act, it simultaneously declared its right to tax the colonies; Parliament suspended the New York legislature for rejecting the taxation implied in the quartering Act; and, in 1767, Parliament imposed duties on all glass, lead, paint, tea, and paper imported by the colonies.

The impact of the Declaratory Act had been ignored in the joy over repeal. But no fortuitous cloud sheltered the suspension of a colonial legislature or the imposition of taxes intended entirely for British North America. In response to these events a Pennsylvania farmer, replete with rural virtues and a liberal education, knowledgeable in English history, its laws and constitution, spoke forth on the theme of humanity and liberty.[52]

More than anything else, the Farmer's Letters brought home the divergent paths taken by Dickinson and Galloway in their interpretations of the British constitution. Galloway had committed himself to the accomplishments won by a century of constitutional warfare which granted sovereignty to Parliament. Dickinson chose a path perhaps best described by the Farmer's own quotation from Corinthians, "The Letter killeth, but the spirit giveth life."[53] He chose to emphasize the substance of the constitution, rather than its form, to paraphrase the settlement of 1689 for eighteenth-century Englishmen in America. It is also apparent that Dickinson's and Galloway's divergent interpretations in many ways paralleled contradictions within the common law itself.

The "Farmer's Letters" made strange bedfellows of the whiggish Coke and the eighteenth-century tory, David Hume. Hume's six-volume History of England provided much ammunition for the view that Englishmen of all persuasions were bound by the vision of the ancient constitution which fostered a spirit of independence and representative government. Hume made these assertions, but with interesting modifications on the theme. He ridiculed the notion that England had pursued a steadfast course toward liberty, and he equally ridiculed "the fables" which whigs conjured up as ancient history.[54] All this was irrelevant to Hume. His cause was the cause of custom and usage. He wrote

> In each of these successive alterations, the only rule of government which is intelligible, or carries any authority with it, is the established practice of the age, and the maxims of administration which are at the time prevalent and universally assented to....An acquaintance with the ancient periods is chiefly useful...by instructing them in the great mixture of accident, which commonly concurs with a small ingredient of wisdom and foresight, in erecting the

complicated fabric of the most perfect government."[55]

Hume did touch many of the bases covered by Coke. He made much of ancient Germans, free, fierce, and independent, who "were more guided by persuasion than authority in the submission which they paid to their princes."[56] Their spirit and arms had conquered Roman despotism, and they had established a free constitution which time, if not enemies, eroded. Certain of their principles they carried to England, especially the limited authority of princes who were subordinate "to the community." However, he, unlike Coke, insisted on the aristocratic composition of that body. Commons, he wrote, had little role in limiting royal power, primarily because the landless had little power. He concluded that Anglo-Saxon government had been "extremely aristrocratical": although it had limited royal authority it gave little weight to the common-folk.[57]

Unlike Coke, Hume emphasized feudalism as "the chief foundation both of the political government and of the jurisprudence established by the Normans in England."[58] Hume, however, did not take the traditional tory position that feudalism in the eleventh century sanctified royal prerogative in the seventeenth century or parliamentary supremacy in the eighteenth century. Instead, he proposed that within feudal institutions there had grown means of securing property for the aristocracy. Hume wrote, "The northern nations had no idea that any man trained up to honor and inured to arms, was ever to be governed, without his consent, by the absolute will of another...."[59] The barons, however, had viewed Parliament ambivalently, both as a privilege and as a burden. "Consent and advice" was their prerogative, but their presence also indicated subordination to the crown, "drew them from that independence which they are apt to affect in their own castles and manors...."[60]

At every opportunity Hume reiterated the aristocratic cast of a Parliament made up of king and council, to the end that the people were not only ignored but exploited. Anglo-Norman government thought little of the unknown masses. Political arrangements revolved about the nebulous balance between royal and baronial prerogatives. Magna Carta made the political lines less nebulous by creating order and explicit standards of government. "Thus," Hume observed, "the establishment of the Great Charter, without seeming anywise to innovate in the distribution of political power, became a kind of epoch in the constitution."[61]

A kind of whig and tory consensus emerged from the precepts of Coke and Hume. They agreed on an ancient English constitution which inclined Englishmen toward principles of liberty. Hume emphasized the aristocratic bias of English guarantees, but the whig Coke went no further than to include freeholders in the ancient law's endowments.

Hume, more than Coke, underlined the growth of law as a process of adaptation. Dickinson's own legal training led him to respect the impact of custom and usage and the haphazard development of common law. Hume warned that common law did not predetermine English government toward liberty. Hume taught that only great vigilance in warding off tyranny and the small incursions which grew into precedents preserved liberty. British history continually described defense against illegal taxation as the most popular political exercise. Dickinson perceived, with Hume's lesson in mind, that as the crown had once threatened England, so Parliament now threatened the colonies. The lessons on liberation learned by the English the Pennsylvania Farmer transmitted to his countrymen.

The Farmer's first letter struck the note of liberation. It was dated November 5, 1767, the anniversary of the day William of Orange landed on the shores of England. From there the analogy grew, but for parliamentary tyranny rather than royal. The problem lay not in Parliament's right to legislate for the colonies, for that was within Parliament's realm. But, Dickinson insisted, parliamentary taxation was without colonial consent, and therefore illegal. He made no distinction between internal and external taxes. The only criterion was that of function. If Parliament passed legislation for the purpose of raising revenue, then that revenue was a tax. Therefore, the Stamp duties, the Townshend duties, and the suspension of the New York legislature were all parts of a single plot to tax the colonists without their consent. The Quartering Act, on whose account New York had been punished, had taxed the colonists in the form of supplies; the Townshend duties were more overt, but its principles differed in no way from those of the earlier stamp duties. All three were illegal attempts to tax the colonies without their consent.

Submitting to taxes levied without consent meant submitting to slavery. History warned of the dangers of precedents which once admitted a right without bounds. Coke, Dickinson pointed out, constantly repeated this theme: "It is a worthy observation," Coke wrote in his second Institute, "how quietly subsidies, granted in forms usual and accustomable (though heavy) are borne: such a power hath use and custom. On the other side, what discontentments and disturbances subsidies framed in a new mold do raise (such an inbred hatred novelty doth hatch) is evident by examples of former times."[62] With subtle deeds Caesar had enslaved Rome, and James II had attempted to enslave England. Similarly, Tacitus had observed, "That which is now supported by examples, growing old, will become an example itself."[63] The Farmer warned, therefore, "behold the ruin hanging over your heads. If you ONCE admit, that Great Britain may lay duties upon her exportations to us, for the purpose of levying money on us only, then she will have nothing to do, but to lay those duties on the articles which she prohibits us to manufacture and the tragedy of American liberty is finished."[64]

If the Glorious Revolution had guaranteed English liberties, it had done so by providing a system of checks and controls by which to prevent tyranny.[65] Among these was the tacit agreement that all taxes were voluntary gifts. Coke assured his readers that taxes could be granted only with the consent of the donors. Edward I, Coke wrote, had agreed that subsidies, parliamentary aids, and customs were voluntary gifts, "for the quieting of the commons, and for a perpetual and constant law for ever after, both in this and other like cases."[66]

England's mixed government demanded a particularly delicate balance of parts because it was "not only mixt, but dependent...."[67] The power of the assemblies provided the prime defense in the vigilance against overextended parliamentary sovereignty. And it was that security which parliamentary legislation had attacked.

Dickinson wrote that assemblies had three main functions: defense, administration of justice, and support of the civil government.[68] To undermine the first power, Parliament had imposed a standing army in time of peace. Rapin, to whom Dickinson frequently turned for historical precedents, had written of a similar attempt by the Stuart tyrant, Charles I. "To make the people in some measure fully sensible of their new slavery," he wrote, "the King affected to muster his forces, which from one regiment of Foot, and one troop of Horseguards... were increased to four thousand completely trained and effective men."[69] And from the Machiavelli of the Discourses, Dickinson learned that Rome fell when the senate turned its power over to the military.[70] Parliament had undermined the second assembly power, the administration of justice, through judicial tenure at the king's pleasure, and by writs of assistance which gave to the same man the power to issue the writs and to judge the defendants. In England, Coke pointed out, only the Court of Exchequer had the privileges to grant writs.[71] Parliament attempted to usurp the last of Dickinson's three assembly functions, support of civil government, by creating a civil list, thereby undermining the assembly's most potent check, the power of the purse. The impact upon colonial liberties was clear. "Is it possible," he asked, "to form an idea of slavery more compleat, more miserable, more disgraceful, than that of a people, where justice is administered, government exercised, and a standing army maintained. AT THE EXPENCE OF THE PEOPLES, and yet WITHOUT THE LEAST DEPENDENCE UPON THEM?"[72]

Americans, Dickinson wrote, would defend their rights as defined in the Bill of Rights, the Stamp Act Resolutions: no taxation without the consent.of their representatives; representation only by their representatives in the assemblies; and the principle of the free gift of supplies.[73] He warned, as he had earlier warned Pitt, that the colonists would revolt "if at length it became UNDOUBTED that an inveterate resolution is formed to annihilate the liberties of the governed...."[74] In less than a decade many colonists became convinced that, indeed, each succeeding British measure would lead to slavery.

Dickinson had alerted Americans to the danger inherent in the legislation passed by Parliament, particularly in matters of taxation. But he had not yet formulated a philosophy of empire with which to refute that legislation. Distinctions between legislation and taxation were only stop-gap remedies for the more deeply rooted problems of empire. Edmund Morgan wrote that the Stamp Act crisis resulted in "well-defined constitutional principles."[75] Further, according to Morgan, from 1765 to 1776, Americans "consistently" made the distinction between taxation (illegal) and legislation (legitimate). Morgan is correct that the Stamp Act crisis finally brought Americans to distinguish between the power to tax and the power to legislate. Colonists had not, however, arrived at a constitutional philosophy with which to support that distinction. The British constitution needed to be brought into the eighteenth century. The Glorious Revolution, upon which parliamentary supremacy rested, had not provided for an empire which did not then exist. Dickinson's writing, cogent and radical for its day, made but tentative probings at the larger problem: the relationship between British colonies in North America in the eighteenth century to a constitutional settlement won by Englishmen in the seventeenth. The ultimate answer, of course, was independence. Americans reached that stage in response to the Coercive Acts and the legal philosophy of empire broached for the English by Sir William Blackstone.

Footnotes

[1] Joseph Galloway to Benjamin Franklin, September 20, 1765, Franklin Papers, XIII, 269. Galloway led a productive group of about 800 people to help defend the house of John Hughes, Pennsylvania's stamp distributor, from the mob. Optimistically, he advised Franklin that "I think Hughes will be able to put his commission in execution, not withstanding the Examples set by the other colonies." Ibid., 270.

[2] Galloway, "Americanus," Pennsylvania Gazette. August 15, 1765. The article is reprinted in pamphlet form in the Evans microcard series: the reference here is to pp. 10-11 of that pamphlet. The series follows the listings in Charles Evans, ed., American Bibliography: A Chronological Dictionary of all Books, Pamphlets and Periodical Publications Printed in the United States...1630...1820 (Chicago, 1903-34) (hereafter cited as Galloway, "Americanus" with page references to the Evans microcard.series).

[3] Ibid., 20.

[4] Ibid.

[5] Galloway to Franklin, October 8-14, 1765, Franklin Papers, XII, 304-05.

[6] Galloway to Franklin, Nov. 16-28, a765, ibid., 376.

[7] Galloway, "Americanus," 21.

[8] He wrote "I am sorry their Conduct upon the whole does not

promise more success then it seems to do. It is ...still more unfortunate that they could not agree to form such addresses as all could sign. I mean Decent and Moderate and not negative of the Parliamentary Jurisdiction...." See Galloway to Franklin, Franklin Papers, XIII, 378.

[9] Ibid., 377.

[10] See Ray F. Harvey, Burlamaqui: A Liberal Tradition in American Constitutionalism (Chapel Hill, 1937) The key to his eclectic appeal is found in the wide spectrum of definitions for the word "happiness."

[11] Jean Jacques Burlamaqui, The Principles of Natural and Political Law, trans. Thomas Nugent (London, 1784), II, Part k, Bk. 8, no. 12; ibid., I, Bk. 10, no. 1. Nugent's First translation appeared in 1748. John Adams, among others, owned a copy.

[12] Ibid., I, Bk. 9, no. 10.

[13] Ibid., Bk. 8, no. 2-4.

[14] Ibid.

[15] Joseph Galloway, Political Reflections on the Late Colonial Government (London, 1783), 2-3.

[16] Ibid., 5.

[17] Ibid., 6

[18] Ibid.

[19] Ibid., 7.

[20] Ibid., 13

[21] Ibid., 24n.

[22] Ibid., 24; Burlamaqui, I, ch. 8, no. 35-36.

[23] Galloway, Political Reflections, 24; Burlamaqui, II, Part I. ch. 8, no. 41.

[24] Galloway, Political Reflections, 28n; Burlamaqui, I, Part I. ch. 7, no. 34.

[25] Galloway, Political Reflections.

[26] Ibid., 21-23.

[27] Ibid., 23.

[28] Ibid., 31.

[29] Ibid., 31-32.

[30] Ibid., 40.

[31] Ibid., 48.

[32] Ibid., 57-58, 63-64.

[33] Ibid., 84-85.

[34] Ibid., 94.

[35] Ibid., 98, 121, 124, 256-59.

[36] John Dickinson, "Stamp Act Resolutions," Writings, 173.

[37] Ibid., 174.

[38] Ibid.

[39] Ibid., 173-74.

[40] Dickinson, "The Declaration of Rights Adopted by the Stamp Act Congress, October, 1765," Writings" 183-87.

[41] Dickinson, "Petition to the King, October 19, 1765," Writings. 193-96.

[42] Dickinson, "Letter to the Committee of Correspondence in

Barbadoes," Writings, 262-63.

[43] Dickinson, "Address to Friends and Countrymen," Writings, 203.

[44] Ibid.

[45] Ibid.

[46] Dickinson to William Pitt, December 21, 1765. Dickinson Papers, Historical Society of Pennsylvania. A more convenient copy is printed in Edmund Morgan, ed., Prologue to Revolution: Sources and Documents on the Stamp Act Crisis. 1764-1766 (Chapel Hill, 1959), 119.

[47] Ibid., 120.

[48] Dickinson, "The Late Regulations Respecting the British Colonies Considered, December 7, 1765," Writings. 213-45.

[49] Ibid., 216-17.

[50] Ibid., 218, 243.

[51] Ibid., 221-22, 243.

[52] Dickinson, "Letters from a Farmer in Pennsylvania," Writings, 307.

[53] Ibid.,347.

[54] David Hume, History of England From the Invasion of Julius Caesar to the Revolution of 1688 (New York, 1859), I, ix-x,l. The first edition was published in 1763, the edition Dickinson must have used; later pre-revolutionary editions were published in 1770 and 1773.

[55] Ibid., II, 514.

[56] *Ibid*., I, 152.

[57] *Ibid*., 152-57.

[58] *Ibid*., 441.

[59] *Ibid*.. 446-47.

[60] *Ibid*.

[61] *Ibid*., 473-74.

[62] Coke, *Institutes*, II, 33; *Farmer's Letters*, 316.

[63] *Ibid*., 346.

[64] *Ibid*., 320.

[65] *Ibid*., 355.

[66] *Ibid*., 329: Coke, *Institutes*, II, 532-33.

[67] *Farmers Letters*, 386.

[68] *Ibid*., 366-67.

[69] Paul Rapin-Thoyras, *The History of England*, trans. N. Tindal (London, 1723), III, 734.

[70] Niccolo Machiavelli, *Discourses on the First Decade of Titus Livius* (London, 1883), Book 3, ch. 24; *Farmer's Letters*, 391-92.

[71] Coke, *Institutes*. IV, 104.

[72] *Farmer's Letters*, 372.

[73] *Ibid*., 331-32.

[74] *Ibid*., 325.

[75] Edmund S. and Helen M. Morgan, *The Stamp Act Crisis' Prologue to Revolution* (New York, 1963), 369-70.

CHAPTER FIVE

THE SECOND STAGE, 1770 to 1775

There were six troubled years between the Revenue Act of 1764 and the repeal of the Townshend duties. Six years more separated the Boston Massacre from the Declaration of Independence. In the first period colonial lawyers had chafed under the ambiguities of the English constitution, until Sir William Blackstone provided the spur to clearer constitutional thinking, as well as the focal point for the colonists' legal argument.

In the years 1765 to 1769 Blackstone published the four volumes of his *Commentaries on the Laws of England*. His purpose was to codify England's laws. No such attempt had been made since the days of Coke's *Institutes* more than a century earlier. Coke's work was ambiguous and needed revision; further, in the era between Coke and Blackstone, England had become an empire. Blackstone undertook to bring England's laws into the eighteenth century.

Blackstone emphasized the timelessness of the English legal tradition: common law had grown by long and immemorial usage, and by their universal reception throughout the kingdom."[1] From the common law sprang "the absolute rights of Englishmen...coeval with our form of government...."[2] To the pantheon of English rights (Magna Carta, the Petition of Rights, and the Habeas Corpus Act) Blackstone added the Bill of Rights of the Glorious

Revolution. These protections, he assured Englishmen, belonged to all natural-born subjects "which their acquire by being born within the king's ligeance, and can never forfeit by any distance of place and time...."[3]

If Blackstone's sentiments on the rights of Englishmen were commendable, they were also commonplace. Why, then, did he draw the full wrath of colonial lawyers? The answer was two-fold. First, he placed the colonists outside his constitutional scheme. Second, he espoused the doctrine of parliamentary omnipotence.

Parliamentary omnipotence and the Bill of Rights marked the gulf between Coke's seventeenth century and Blackstone's eighteenth. Whereas Coke had lived in an age when constitutional reformers sought to limit royal prerogative by extorting privileges for the legislature, Blackstone's England presumed that the constitutional quarrel had been resolved. The Bill of Rights sealed the Glorious Revolution. The voice of Parliament replaced hereditary claim and divine right; essentially, Englishmen paid homage to the Crown of England, rather than to the king's person. Blackstone's definition of Parliament's role made dogma out of the political reality of his day.

Blackstone touched the nerve of eighteenth-century English constitutional thinking when he identified parliamentary sovereignty with the rule of law. "Law," Blackstone wrote early in his first volume, is "that rule of action which is prescribed by some superior, and which the inferior is bound to obey."[4]

Parliament (king, lords, and commons) made tangible the functions of that superior power. "Sovereignty and legislature," he added, "are indeed convertible terms: one cannot subsist without the other....legislature...is the greatest act of sovereignty that can be exercised by one being over another."[5] By equating parliamentary supremacy with constitutionalism Blackstone helped shore up England's increasingly adamant position toward the colonies; on the other side of the Atlantic colonial lawyers heard only the loud voice of authority conclude: "So long, therefore, as the English constitution lasts, we may venture to affirm that the power of Parliament is absolute and without control."[6]

Englishmen welcomed parliamentary power because its basic premise was the rights of Englishmen. Blackstone, however, restricted the applicability of those rights to what he called "this island."[7] In effect, then, the constitutional settlement obtained by the Glorious Revolution did not apply to the colonies, even had they wished it.

Indeed, Blackstone wrote specifically on colonial subjugation. The American "plantation," he said, was either "conquered or ceded." Although colonists carried with them the English laws of their day, they did so only insofar as these applied to the colonial status, that is, rules of inheritance and personal protection. Irrelevant mercantile regulations, for example, did not follow them. Successive generations might adopt specific English regulations "but then it received its obligation and authoritative force form being the law of the [colonial] country."[8] On this point Blackstone was clear: "the common law of England, as such, has no allowance or authority there, they [colonies] being no part of the mother-country, but distinct (though dependent) dominions. They are subject, however, to the control of Parliament...."[9] He added that Americans, like the Irish, were bound only by those parliamentary acts which specifically named them.[10]

The Irish question provided an important precedent for American colonial lawyers. In many ways Ireland and Americans suffered similar restrictions. Blackstone considered Ireland also a conquered and dependent province subservient to the "crown of England."[11] Charles H. McIlwain argues that the Declaratory Act for Ireland in 1719 (6 Geo. I) and the Declaratory Act of 1766, which was coupled with the repeal of the Stamp Act, involved identical constitutional questions. If the Act of 1719 was valid, as R. L. Schuyler argued in return, then the American bill had similar authority. American lawyers, of course, denied the legitimacy of either measure. They countered that the Irish condition did not prevent its Parliament from controlling important internal affairs. As a "distinct dominion" (to use Blackstone's phrase) Ireland possessed common law guarantees, its own Parliament, power over taxation, and the right to legislate in areas ignored by England. Although the latter insisted on its supremacy over Ireland, American lawyers contended it also recognized the legitimate dominion of the body to which Irishmen sent their representatives.[12] The Irish example, then, provided a possible alternative for those colonists who sought release from British taxation without simultaneously rejecting Parliament's authority.

Galloway's Plan of Union (1774) must be considered in that category. Galloway made the supremacy of Parliament his underlying premise. But a close look at the structure he proposed reveals that in practice he inclined toward equality within the empire. For example, his Plan provided for a Grand Council, representative of the colonial assemblies, which would speak for the colonies in all affairs involving them with Great Britain; further, the Council's veto power over all colonial legislation denied to Parliament the power of unilateral legislation for the colonies. Galloway's Plan of Union went far beyond the meek acceptance of English rule.

Although James Wilson and John Dickinson became spokesmen for more radical views, they, too, sought their alternatives from within the English constitutional heritage. But they left the middle road by rejecting the finality of the Glorious Revolution. In their eyes (and in Blackstone's) the Revolution had produced parliamentary supremacy; colonists saw that supremacy as a tyranny as great as that of the Stuarts. Wilson and Dickinson sought alternatives, in the fashion of lawyers, in precedents from within England's past. Their counter-constitutionalism replaced the legislative authority of king, lords, and commons, with the older, feudal concept of allegiance to the king's person. In essence, they turned to Coke for precedents of feudal relationships which bypassed Parliament but retained the protection of a contractual relationship inherent in the whig theory of government. In reality, theirs was a monarchy royal rather than a monarchy seignorial (to use Dickinson's distinction) designed to moderate the uncontrolled and impersonal authority of Parliament with the benign and limited power of mythic feudalism.

The Coercive or Intolerable Acts (1774) made blatant Parliament's claims to sovereignty over the colonies. Americans could no longer shield themselves from the impact of Blackstone's assertion of sovereignty by the victors of 1688. On one essential point Galloway, Wilson, and Dickinson agreed: as the empire was then structured, parliamentary dominion was inconsistent with the rights of Englishmen.

ii

In 1768, just three years out of Scotland, James Wilson wrote _Consideration on the Nature and Extent of the Legislative Authority of the British Parliament_. It was less than a year since he had studied law in Dickinson's office. The Pennsylvania Farmer's reputation was then at its peak for denouncing Parliament's attempt to tax the colonies. Wilson let his pamphlet lie unpublished. In 1774, the Intolerable Acts provided the more propitious moment for its publication. In that same year, John Dickinson published _An_

Essay on the Constitutional Power of Great Britain over the Colonies in America, which denied to Parliament not only the right to tax, but also the right to legislate for the colonies "in every instance."[13]

Blackstone, of course, was the prime villain. Parliamentary supremacy was contrary to Wilson's view of "the principles of justice and freedom, and of the British constitution." His basic premise was shared by the Pennsylvania Farmer: rights implied equality. Colonists had neither unless they controlled Parliament to the extent which it was controlled by other Englishmen. "Can the Americans," Wilson asked, "who are descended from British ancestors, and inherit all their rights, be blamed -- can they be blamed _by their brethren in Britain_ -- for claiming still to enjoy these rights? But can they enjoy them, if they are bound by the acts of a British parliament?"[14] Wilson's task was to define the nature of "equality" and to apply that criterion to the imperial structure based on parliamentary supremacy.

From Burlamaqui, Wilson adopted the assumption that the first test of government is the happiness of the governed.[15] Burlamaqui had argued further that the civil liberty of the individual required "a right of insisting upon their [sovereign power] making a good use of their authority, and with a moral security that this right will have its effect."[16] Wilson examined parliamentary supremacy in the light of these criteria of security and happiness and asked:

> Will it ensure and increase the happiness of the American colonies,that the parliament of Great Britain should possess a supreme, irresistible, uncontrolled authority over them? Is such an authority consistent with their liberty? Have they any security that it will be employed only for their own good? Such a security is absolutely necessary.[17]

Wilson borrowed many of his suspicions of parliamentary rule from Henry St. John Bolingbroke, the eighteenth-century tory and defender of balanced government. Wilson relied especially on Bolingbroke's "Dissertation upon Parties," dedicated to Sir Robert Walpole, in which Bolingbroke underscored the high probability of corruption inherent in an uncontrolled Parliament.[18] The theory of a balanced government, Bolingbroke wrote, presupposes that "our kings may abuse their power, and our representatives betray their trust, and provides against both these contingencies, as well as human wisdom can provide."[19] "A bad king," he observed, "must stand in awe of an honest parliament."[20] His major concern, however, was with the newer problem of a corrupt and powerful Commons.

The only sure method of controlling Parliament's natural inclinations toward self-interest, Bolingbroke advised, was through frequent elections of its membership. A short hold on great power provided the only surety against excess. In terms which Wilson frequently paraphrased, Bolingbroke insisted that the power of the electorate was essential to keeping parliamentary power within its legitimate boundaries: "frequent elections of the representatives, by the collective body of the people, in order to secure. the latter against the ill consequences of the possible weakness or corruption of the former... [is a] fundamental...article, and essential to the preservation of our liberties."[21]

Wilson accepted the exhortations of Burlamaqui and Bolingbroke that a free people maintains its freedom only as long as it controls political authority. Englishmen, Wilson wrote, had established channels by which to restrain Parliament. He agreed that the most important of these ("the strongest bulwark of the British liberties") was the right of election. Further, Englishmen could rely on frequent elections, by which "the constitution is...frequently renewed, and drawn back, as it were, to its first principles,...The first maxims of jurisprudence are ever kept in view that their happiness is the end of government."[22] Other, less tangible factors aided Englishmen; for example, they shared with their representatives a common interest in the welfare of the country. Wilson observed, "Every measure, that is prejudicial to the nation, must be prejudicial to them and their posterity. They cannot betray their electors without, at the same time, injuring themselves."[23] Finally, Englishmen, unlike colonists, possessed the "power of the purse" which, in the guise of gifts to the sovereign, remained the most obvious constitutional check.[24]

The right of representation gave Parliament its authority. The power of election, frequent elections, the power of the purse, and the community of interest which bound members of Parliament to the people, saved Englishmen from the tyranny of an independent sovereign power. Wilson underscored the fact that none of these controls was available to the colonists; neither election, nor power of the purse, nor community of interest bound Parliament to Englishmen in North America. Further, their interests might well be contradictory. Wilson concluded that without the securities cherished by Englishmen, colonists could not grant the power of unlimited sovereignty to Parliament. In one of the strongest statements of his essay, Wilson summarized his position, saying:

> But are the representatives of the commons of Great Britain the representatives of the Americans? Are they elected by Americans? Are they such as the Americans, if they had the power of election, would probably elect? Do they know the interest of the Americans? If they do not pursue it, have the Americans power to punish them? Can the Americans remove unfaithful members at every new election? Can members, whom Americans do not elect; with whom the Americans are not connected in interest; whom the Americans cannot remove; over whom the Americans have no influence -- can such members by styled, with any propriety, the magistrates of the Americans?[25]

Wilson, of course, answered in the negative. He wrote:

> It is repugnant to the essential maxims of jurisprudence, to the ultimate end of all governments, to the genius of the British constitution, and to the liberty and happiness of the colonies, that they should be bound by the legislative authority of the parliament of Great Britain....the colonies are not bound by the acts of the British parliament; because they have no share in the British legislature.[26]

Wilson concluded this theme by pointing to the example of Ireland. Although Irishmen were subjects of the King, their own Parliament legislated for them. "Our statues do not bind them," he gloated, "Because they do not send knights to Parliament."[27].

Although Wilson's statement ranks among the most coherent of arguments against parliamentary power in the colonies, by 1774 others had reached similar conclusions.[28] John Dickinson responded to the Intolerable Acts with An Essay on the Constitutional Power of Great Britain over the Colonies in America, in which he firmly agreed with Wilson.

Colonial problems with the British constitution, Dickinson wrote, lay in its ambivalence; nowhere was there a positive statement of American authority. Britain's resolution of the problem came from two sources: Blackstone and Parliament. Blackstone's Commentaries described the constitution as a restriction on royal rather than parliamentary prerogatives; Parliament agreed to its own omnipotence. Dickinson commented: "True it is that it has been solemnly declared by parliament that parliament has such a power."[29] Dickinson concluded that the English solved the constitutional ambivalence by assuming that "Because the constitution has not "expressly declared the line between the rights of the mother country and those of her colonists," Therefore, the latter. have no rights."[30]

Dickinson proposed an alternative standard that decisions determining constitutional boundaries be based on "the happiness of the people in the end..."[31] On that basis he proposed to evaluate recent British legislation, especially the Massachusetts Government Act, extension of admiralty jurisdiction, and change of venue, which he charged infringed upon the right of habeas corpus.[32] "The matter is brought to this single point," Dickinson wrote, "whether taking our money from us without our consent, depriving us of trial by jury, changing constitutions of government, and abolishing the privilege of the writ of habeas corpus, by seizing and carrying us to England, have no greater tendency to diminish our happiness than any enormities a King can commit under pretence of prerogative can have to diminish the happiness of the subjects in England."[33]

Parliament, in his view, posed the greatest danger to the happiness of the people, primarily because the colonists had no means of controlling its power. Neither did the colonists share mutual interests with the British which would shape legislation. On the contrary, in matters of taxation it would benefit the British to exploit colonists, against which the latter would have no recourse. "Can man give and grant what they have not? Did any of those acts take a single penny out of the pockets of a single giver and grantor?" Dickinson added, "Statutes might grind us, while not an elector would know or regard our sufferings -- if acquainted with them, he might think the statutes inflicting them, just and political.[34]

As a lawyer, Dickinson knew how quickly statute took on the dignity of precedent. Within a decade parliament had dipped into a wide range of America's internal affairs. Dickinson listed them: religion, taxation, admiralty courts, trial by jury, standing armies, civil lists, and the basic constitutional structure.[35] These measures "give rise to many alarming apprehensions in Americ.....Power debauches the affections.... If she Great Britain affixed no limits on her power, why should we affix any to its effects."[36] Parliaments's actions in exercising its claim of unlimited legislative power over colonial America led Dickinson to conclude, as did Wilson, that "the just inference... would be an exclusion of any power over these colonies, rather than an admission of unbounded power."[37]

By the summer of 1774, John Dickinson and James Wilson had separately reached the conclusion that Parliament's power to legislate was based on its representative obligations; where it had none, neither had it the power to legislate. That conclusion, however, did not sever America's ties with England. Although the colonies were not subordinate to a Parliament which did not represent them, Wilson argued, they remained part of the British empire through their loyalties to the king's person and his protection.

Wilson contended that "allegiance to the king and obedience to the parliament are founded on very different principles. The former is founded on protection...."[38] Wilson's assumption that the power of the king and the power of Parliament were divisible was ar anachronism in the eighteenth century. The Glorious Revolution had made it clear that the Crown drew its political strength from its conjunction with the Lords and Commons in Parliament.[39] Further, Wilson ascribed to the relationship between king and subject qualities reminiscent of the mythic feudalism supported by Coke and the whig tradition.[40] These connections were understandable, because outside of Ireland's relationship with England, Wilson drew mainly upon Calvin's Case (1608) or Postnati, in which Coke played a major role.

The details of the case are straightforward. Robert Calvin, a Scottish alien, was born in the third year of the reign of James I. In 1608, his guardians sued to have Calvin declared a naturalized Englishman, which would enable Calvin to inherit English property. James, hoping to encourage mutual naturalization, used Postnati as a test case with which to gauge the sentiment of the Commons.[41]

The pivotal question in Calvin's Case concerned the nature of allegiance: did a subject pay homage to the laws of the land or to the person of the king? Feudal theory had blurred these distinctions between the sovereign and the laws; allegiance to the sovereign implied no obedience to laws of any dominion outside the subjects' own. Nationalism had creating conflicting loyalties to a new creature, the "body politic."[42]

Calvin's opponents supported the new concept of loyalty. They argued that the King of Scotland and the King of England possessed separate political personages in each kingdom. "In the king's person," the defendants claimed, "there concur two distinct and several kingdoms: therefore it is all one as if they are in divers persons' and consequently the plaintiff is an alien, as all the antenati are, for that they are born under the ligeance of another King."[43] A citizen of Scotland owed obedience, they claimed, to the laws and the Crown of Scotland alone and had no obligations to England, nor was he subject to English laws. Therefore, "every subject that is born out of the extent and reach of the laws of England, cannot by judgement of those laws be a natural subject to the King, in respect to his kingdoms of England...."[44]

On Calvin's side, the plaintiff's lawyers argued for the traditional view of allegiance. "Ligeance is a true and faithful obedience of the subject due to his Sovereign," they argued. "This ligeance and obedience is an incident inseparable to every subject: for as soon as he is born he oweth by birthright ligeance and obedience to his Sovereign." They underscored their basically feudal perspective by comparing the ties of king and subject to those of lord and tenant: "for as the subject oweth to the King his true and faithful ligeance and obedience, so the sovereign is to govern and protect his subjects...."[45] Therefore, the subject's loyalties to his king transcended political and geographic distinctions. Englishmen and Scotsmen shared mutual obligations to James. As a result, they were not alien to each other but jointly subJects of the King."[46] Although Scotland held to its own body of laws and to its own Parliament, it shared with England a king and, therefore, common naturalization. Coke's decision for Calvin in 1608 provided an important precedent with which to challenge Parliament's claim that recognition of its legislative supremacy was a pre-condition to membership in the British empire.[47]

Wilson had been drawn to Calvin's Case by his belief that Parliament, rather than the King, posed the greater threat to American liberties.48 In 1775, called upon to defend the legality of the Continental Congress, Wilson abandoned his idealization of the monarchy. "The distinction between him [George III] and his ministers has been lost," Wilson admitted, "but they have not been raised to his situation, he has sunk to theirs."[49] For many the king had provided the last feasible tie of empire. They soon realized that the next step was independence.

The role of legal training in predisposing colonial lawyers toward loyalism or patriotism in the struggle with Great Britain is, of course, the important issue. The pivotal question turned on the king's role as a political or a private figure, the Crown or the king. Patriots, like Wilson, had no alternative but independence when that distinction collapsed. Galloway, ultimately a loyalist who thought the distinction between Parliament and the King absurd, found shelter in his plan to restructure the empire upon the parliamentary foundation which he continued to find legitimate.

Galloway's Plan of Union awkwardly straddled the British and American cause: he found it impossible to support "the distinction between King and Crown, yet he agreed that the colonies were not properly represented in Parliament. He hoped that by solving the latter problem there would be no need for the former. To that end, he proposed a new "British and American legislature" which would permit each colony control over its internal affairs and a voice in matters affecting colonial America and Great Britain.

The proposed new legislature consisted of a Grand Council and a President General. Members of the Grand Council would be chosen by colonial assemblies for three year terms; the Council would meet yearly, choose its own Speaker, and enjoy all the privileges possessed by the House of Commons. Galloway also proposed an executive officer, the President General, to be appointed by the King. The President General was to hold veto power over acts of the Council, and he, "by and with the Advice and Consent of the Grand Council," would regulate affairs affecting more than one colony or the colonies and Great Britain. The plan required both American and British consent for all legislation affecting the colonies, with one exception. In time of war, the colonists alone would decide the amount of their financial aid to Britain. Finally, the President General and the Grand Council constituted "an inferior and distinct Branch of the British Legislature.[50] In essence, Galloway proposed to give Americans official standing in the British empire, a real voice in legislation through their elected representatives, and security of property, which he considered the basis of all government. Galloway's ambivalence toward the constitutional arguments at hand was nowhere more apparent than in his little-known essay, "An Argument on Both Sides in the Dispute Between Great Britain and her Colonies," which he wrote as a private commentary on his Plan of Union."[51] The essay was Galloway's attempt to clarify for himself the validity of British and American arguments.

The British case rested on parliamentary supremacy and the

nature of the Crown. All forms of government, Galloway wrote, required a source of supreme authority; in Britain's mixed form of government, that supreme authority rested with Parliament. Galloway shared Blackstone's view that the colonies had come to England through conquest or discovery and, therefore, they were part of England's realm and subject to its legislation.[52] Furthermore, Galloway added, no exemption from Parliament's authority could come from the King, "because the territory granted was not the private Property of the Grantor or King executive, but of the Crown, or King, Lords and Commons, as the Representatives and Trustees of the Nation, in whom alone the supreme Power of the whole state is vested."[53]

Galloway concluded, on the British side, that in relationship with the colonies, no valid distinction could be made between King and Crown. King, lords, and commons provided the focal point of supreme authority for the English realm. He wrote:

> Upon these arguments, drawn from the established Principles of all Governments, from the Necessity of a supreme power to order, direct and regulate every Member and Part of them, from original Right and Property in the Territory of the Colonies, from the Allegiance due from the People before their Migration! from the Nature of their Charters, and from the Necessity resulting from their present disunited situation, the British Government derive their Claim to bind the Colonies in all Cases whatever.[54]

On those same grounds, however, Galloway found equal justification for American complaints. He disdained the distinctions with which colonists (Dickinson, in particular) had played from 1765 to 1770 -- taxation and legislation, regulation of trade and revenue -- dismissing them as "Distractions...with

Respect to American rights....I have searched for them in the common law in the usage and customs of England -- in the Volumes of the Statutes -- and in the Laws and Journals of Parliament-- and they are not to be found...."[55]

It was not surprising that Galloway dismissed the arguments of his long-time foe, John Dickinson. Galloway's anguish grew from his conviction that the grounds which he considered "more safe and defensible...the Constitution of the English Government, and the Principles and Policy upon which it is founded," supported colonial charges of legislative tyranny.[56]

It was an ironic admission from the man who, in 1776, would join General Howe as a loyalist, that the British stance was a superficial one. This point is so important in Galloway's career that his statement must be quoted in its entirety:

> On the other Side then it may be asserted in Favor of America, that altho' the Facts advanced against her may be true, and the Arguments drawn from these Principles may be just, yet taking the Subject deeper, and tracing the Policy upon which the English Constitution was established, and bringing into View the Security and Freedom which was intended by that Policy to be ensured to the Governed, to every Member of the State, it will appear that Parliament ought not, as the Colonies are at present circumstanced, to bind them by its Legislative Authority.[57]

Galloway's thoughts followed the pattern developed by James Wilson and John Dickinson. The right of legislation, Galloway wrote, rested with those who represented property holders, the source of English political power; Lords and Commons represented those who held land "within the Realm." "Hence the ancient Maxim, That no Laws are binding save those which are made with the Consent of the whole Nation. i.e. of the Proprietors of all the Lands within the Realm."[58] "Time immemorial" supported this claim, Galloway wrote. In ancient Saxon days property owners personally participated in the legislative process; feudal tradition obligated landowners to attend feudal courts; even William the Conqueror, Galloway insisted, continued the process by which men who owned land "held and exercised a Share in the supreme Legislature."[59] The right of any landowning Englishman to participate in the legislative process through their representative was, in Galloway's eyes, "the Essence of the English Government," and representation provided the "Great and only Check upon arbitrary Power, the great Bulwark against Tyranny and Oppression, and the main Pillar and support of the Freedom and Liberties of the English Subject."[60]

"No Part or Spot of the Lands in America. or the Owners and Proprietors thereof," were represented in the Parliament of Great Britain. That omission, Galloway warned, left his countrymen in America defenseless against tyranny. No patriot could have concluded as earnestly as Galloway that without proper representation "the British Government is as absolute and despotic, with respect to the colonies, as any Monarchy or despotic Government whatever, in as much as the Persons, Lives, and Estates of their Inhabitants, is at the Disposal of a Power according to its Will and Pleasure in which it has no Voice or Participation.[61]

As similar as Galloway's conclusion might sound to that of

Wilson and Dickinson, it stemmed from a different premise. Galloway believed in the supremacy of king, lords, and commons over all the realm; but subservience to its sovereignty implied that in return the colonists receive full rights and privileges of Englishmen. Galloway believed that the new legislature proposed in the Plan of Union would provide colonial America "not only... [with] the Names but the substantial Rights of Members secured in their ancient Liberties and Freedom...."[62]

The Continental Congress ignored Galloway's Plan of Union, even wiped it from its records. In later days, when Galloway lived in England as an unhappy exile, he bitterly described his opponents as men who had used every "fiction, falsehood and fraud" to bring Americans to revolution.[63] His bitterness and rigidity became increasingly apparent after the events of 1774. Early in the next year, Galloway published a defense of his by-then defunct Plan, a _Candid Examination of the Mutual Claims of Great Britain and the Colonies_....in which he sacrificed the spirit of compromise to the hard lines of his own experience.[64]

A _Candid examination_ is much less coherent and effective than the earlier essay because it was caught in the contradictions of Galloway's own life. He was embittered by the Congress' casual disdain of the Plan which he saw as the panacea for the British empire. He responded with greater rigidity and support for the British constitutional argument. He also clung to his idea for a British and American legislature; to achieve that end he was forced to recognize weaknesses within the British empire. Galloway was torn between punishment and forgiveness; therefore, it is understandable that both permeated A _Candid Examination_.[65]

Galloway found in John Locke, the titular spokesman for the Glorious Revolution, an ally in defense of parliamentary supremacy. Locke had written:

> the first _fundamental positive law_ of all commonwealths is, the establishing of the _legislative power_. This legislative is not only the _supreme power of the commonwealth_; but is sacred and unalterable in the hands where the community have placed it...there can be but one _supreme power_, which is the _legislative_, to which _all the rest are_, and must be SUBORDINATE.[66]

Locke, of course, had supported a revolution designed to limit royal prerogative. It is no surprise that he provided a useful and respected source for limiting the king to political functions of the legislature. Locke wrote:

> The oaths of allegiance are taken to the King; it is not to him as supreme legislator, but as _supreme executor of the law._ made by a joint power of him and others; allegiance being nothing but _obedience according to law_, which when he violates, he has no right to obedience, nor can _claim it_ otherwise than in his _public person_, vested with the _power of the law_.[67]

Galloway patterned his conclusions on Locke. The supreme legislative power, he wrote, rested with king, lords, and commons, of which the king was only first of three, and not supreme. The king had no independent legislative capacity to which the colonists could turn.[68] If Americans claimed to be subjects of the King of Great Britain, then they must recognize the authority of British laws. The only alternative to submission or complete independence was his Plan of Union.[69]

It is worthy of note that neither the loyalist, Galloway, nor the patriots, Wilson and Dickinson, accepted Blackstone's exclusion of colonial Americans from the rights and privileges of Englishmen. Galloway's views more closely paralleled the eighteenth-century English concept of government: the supremacy of Parliament and the "body politic" nature of the Crown. But Galloway insisted, well into exile, that recognition of parliamentary supremacy obligated Parliament, in turn, to recognize the rights of colonial America to the extent of reforming the legislative process. Wilson and Dickinson met the challenge to American rights with another perspective. They rejected Parliament as a tool of tyranny, turned to a mythic image of the king to redress the balance of power. That their experiment in precedent was impractical and futile we know, because by 1776, they rejected that stance in favor of a "body politic" of their own. They had come full-circle to a political and legal philosophy which mimicked the British structure but in a new setting.

It is necessary to point out, also, that these three men, all lawyers, operated within the English legal tradition. They appealed not to amorphous deities but to English cases, statutes and the principles of government to which other Englishmen, a century earlier, had appealed with similar results.

Footnotes

[1] Sir William Blackstone, Commentaries on the Laws of England (New York, 1856), I, 63 (original pagination).

[2] Ibid., 127-28.

[3] Ibid., 370.

[4] Ibid., 38.

[5] Ibid., 46.

[6] Ibid., 161.

[7] Ibid., 50. Blackstone added that the "kingdom of England" excluded Wales, Scotland, Ireland "or any other part of the king's dominions, except the territory of England only." ibid., 93.

[8] Ibid., 106-109.

[9] Ibid., 107-08.

[10] Ibid.

[11] Ibid., 99, 103. The question of allegiance to the crown became important when Wilson attacked that premise in: his Considerations.

[12] The Irish precedent was a dubious blessing. Blackstone cited an act of 20 Hen. VI which provided "a tax granted by the Parliament of England shall not bind those of Ireland, because they are not summoned to our Parliament," ibid., 101. However, he also pointed to Poying's Laws (10 Hen. VII) which protested England's jurisdiction: the Irish Parliament could not consider acts which

had not been reviewed previously by the king. Essentially, the Irish Parliament was limited to veto power. Poyning's Laws did say that no acts of the English Parliament affected Ireland unless specifically stated. The act of 6 Geo. I reiterated England's jurisdiction over Ireland, including legislation and appellate jurisdiction. These acts were not repealed until 1783. See C. H. McIlwain, The American Revolution: A Constitutional Interpretation (Ithaca, 1923), 50-55; Robert Livingston Schuyler, Parliament and the British Empire: Some Constitutional Controversies Concerning Imperial Legislative Jurisdiction (New York, 1929), 89-91.

[13] See John Dickinson, ."Essay on the Constitutional Power of Great Britain over the Colonies in America, 1774," in Pennsylvania Archives. 2d Ser., III, 575 (hereafter cited as Essay). Also, James Wilson, "Considerations on the Nature and Extent of the Legislative Authority of the British Parliament," in McCloskey, Works, II, 721 (hereafter cited as Considerations). The modern edition reissues the three-volume edition published in 1804 by Bird Wilson, son of James. James DeWitt Andrews edited and published a shorter version in 1898. Page references are to McCloskey's edition.

[14] Wilson, Considerations, 11, 722-23, 731.

[15] Ibid.' 723. Wilson further quoted Burlamaqui as saying "the right of sovereignty is that of commanding finally -- but in order to procure real felicity: for if this end is not obtained, sovereignty ceases to be a legitimate authority."

16 Ibid.

17 Ibid., 723-24.

18 Henry St. John Bolingbroke, "Dissertation upon Parties," Works, II, 5-172 (hereafter cited as Parties).

19 Ibid.. 106-07.

20 Ibid., 118. Wilson quoted Bolingbroke as writing also "Thus our constitution supposes that princes may abuse their power, and parliaments betray their trust; and provides, as far as human wisdom can provide, that they may not be able to do so long, without a sufficient control." ibid., 100; See Wilson, Considerations, II, 724.

21 Bolingbroke, Parties, 100-02. Wilson found proof of Bolingbroke's relevance in the Long Parliament of 1640. He concluded a long tirade on its corruption with the admonition that "long parliaments will naturally forget their dependence on the people: when this dependence is forgotten, they will become corrupt." Wilson,Considerations, 728-29. Montesquieu completed the thought with: "Whenever they become corrupt, the constitution of England will lose its liberty it will perish." Spirit of the Laws, Bk. II, ch. 6. Quoted in ibid.

22 Ibid., 726.

23 Ibid., Wilson placed great emphasis on the impact of community of interest and life style: "Having no interest contrary to that of the people, from among whom they were chosen, and with whom, after the session, they were again to mix, they had no views

inconsistent with the liberty of their constituents, and therefore would have no motives to betray it." ibid., 730.

[24] Ibid., 727. Wilson quoted Bacon's Abridgement of the Law (1568) that "No freeman can be taxed at pleasure." Ibid., 730-31.

[25] Ibid., 732.

[26] Ibid., 735.

[27] Ibid. Wilson rejected more restrictive aspects of Ireland's situation: Parliament's right to name Ireland in specific legislation and the judicial process by which the King's bench in Ireland appealed to the King's bench in England. ibid., 737.

[28] See Randolph G. Adams, Political Ideas of the American Revolution: Britannic-American Contributions to the Problem of Imperial Organization 1765 to 1775 (North Carolina, 1922), 53. He writes that Wilson's essay was superior to those of Adams and Jefferson for "clearness of vision, accuracy of analysis, or consistency of presentation."

[29] Dickinson, Essay, 565-68.

[30] Ibid., 569.

[31] Ibid., 566-67.

[32] Ibid.

[33] Ibid., 567.

[34] Ibid., 573n. Dickinson also pointed out that some, if not all, Englishmen had representation. No colonist was represented. Englishmen had no alternatives but their Parliament; colonists could turn to local assemblies. ibid.

[35] Ibid., 582-85.

[36] Ibid., 585-86n. Dickinson drew support for his fear of unlimited taxation and standing armies from English history. On ship money, Dickinson quoted from Lord Clarendon's History, in which Clarendon had warned:

> It is not that ship-money hath been levied upon us, but it is, that thereby ship-money is claimed, which is the gift and the earnest penny of all we have; it is not, that our persons have been imprisoned, for the payment of ship-money but that our persons and lives are, upon the same ground of law, delivered up to will and pleasure. It is that our birthright is destroyed and there hath been an endeavor to reduce us to a lower state than villainage." Quoted in ibid., 595n.

From a less likely patriot, General Gage, commander of all the British troops in North America, Dickinson learned of the dangers of a standing army. Gage, in 1739, had warned Parliament against permitting such a body in England, saying:

> So great a body of troops being kept on foot in England, will be the finishing stroke to all our liberties. For as the towns in England...will be as so many fortresses with strong garrisons in them, erected in all parts of England, which can tend to nothing, but by decrees to subdue and enslave the kingdom.

Gave concluded with the advice that:

> If ever this scheme should be attempted, it will be incumbent on every Englishman to endeavor to prevent it by all methods, and...it would be our duty to draw our swords and never put them up till our liberties were secured and the authors of our intended slavery brought to condign punishment. ibid., 583n.

[37] Ibid., 575.

[38] Wilson, Considerations. 736-37.

[39] George Burton Adams, Constitutional History of England (London, 1928), 362-82.

[40] Wilson expanded on this theme, adding "the colonists ought

to be dependent on the king, because they have hitherto enjoyed, and still enjoy, his protection. Allegiance is the faith and obedience which every subject owes to his prince. This obedience is founded on the protection derived from government....for protection and allegiance are the reciprocal bonds, which connect the prince and his subjects." ibid., 743.

41 Sir Edward Coke, Reports (London, 1826), IV, Part 7, 1-Q: T. B. Howell, a Complete Collection of State Trials (London, 1816), II, 559.

42 Charles H. McIlwain, American Revolution. 92-95. William H. Dunham, Jr., "Doctrines of Allegiance in Late Medieval English Law," New York University Law Review, XXVI (1951), 41. Dunham points out that "the subjects' attachment to the monarch's person was in medieval England...the essence of allegiance." Max Savelle, "Nationalism and Other Loyalties in the American Revolution," American Historical Review, LXVII (1962), 901. Savelle wrote concerning nationalism: "this peculiar form of loyalty did not become a major.factor in the history of the Western world until about the middle of the eighteenth century."

43 Coke, Reports, 4-5.

44 Ibid., 5.

45 Ibid., 8.

46 Ibid., 9.

47 Wilson, Considerations. 744. McIlwain pointed out that Wilson's interpretation of Calvin's Case was questionable. Lord

Chancellor Ellesmere feared the "new" distinction between the king and kingdom. Coke underscored that theme: Allegiance, he argued, "was due to the natural person of the king (which is ever accompanied with the political capacity), and it is not due to the political capacity only, that is, to his crown or kingdom distinct from his natural capacity...." Howell, State Trials. II, 690; Coke, Reports, IV, 17; McIlwain, 204-05. Wilson's interpretation sacrificed the real feudal quality of Coke's decision to make it applicable to a political climate in which the king's power was tied to that of Parliament

48 Wilson, Considerations, 745. Wilson concluded his essay, saying "the connexion and harmony between Great Britain and us...will be better preserved by.the operation of the legal prerogatives of the Crown, than by the execution of an unlimited authority by parliament."

49 Wilson, "Speech Delivered in the Convention for the Province of Pennsylvania, January 1775," Works, II, 758.

50 Joseph Galloway, "Plan of Union, 1774," reprinted in Julian Boyd, Anglo-American Union: Joseph Galloway's Plans to Preserve the British Empire, 1775-1788 (Philadelphia, 1941), 112-14. Galloway submitted his Plan to Congress on September 28, 1774, but it was ordered left out of the Minutes. A draft of the Plan in the Library of Congress indicates that Galloway envisioned numerous benefits resulting from its implementation: a uniform system of government patterned after the British constitution, an efficient

executive power, protection of the rights and privileges of Englishmen and, dear to his heart, an improved judiciary. He hoped that higher salaries would improve the quality of bench and bar. "Plan of Union," Galloway Papers, Library of Congress, 1-4, 13.

[51] Galloway, "Arguments on Both Sides in the Dispute Between Great Britain and her Colonies, 1774," New Jersey Archives, 1st. ser., X, 478-93.

[52] Ibid., 478-79.

[53] Ibid., 480. Galloway reiterated the argument, first apparent in his debate with Dickinson during Pennsylvania's charter crisis, that the legislature's role was to preserve government, not to dissolve it; therefore, any action which undermined its legitimate authority was unconstitutional. For example, to have given the king such power as the colonists claimed for him, Galloway argued, "would enable the King to divide the English Realm into as many petty States as he pleased, and discharge the whole People of Great Britain from the obedience to the Government, and thereby dissolve the Constitution." ibid.

[55] Ibid., 484.

[56] Ibid., 484-85.

[57] Ibid., 485.

[58] Ibid., 485-87.

[59] Ibid.

[60] Ibid., 488.

[61] Ibid.

[62] Ibid., 491.

[63] Galloway, Historical and Political Reflections on The Rise and Progress of the American Rebellion (London, 1780), 66. A copy may be found in the Historical Society of Pennsylvania.

[64] Galloway, a Candid Examination of the Mutual Claims of Great Britain and the Colonies: With a Plan of Accommodation on Constitutional Principles (New York, 1775). Reprinted in London in 1780.

[65] Merrill Jensen is partially responsible for the black and white interpretation of Galloway's position. Jensen quotes from Galloway's Historical and Political Reflections... to prove that "since 1765, (Galloway) consistently upheld the right of Parliament to legislate for the colonies." Jensen concluded, for some reason, that "his comments in the Congress, published in 1780, though biased, represent his feelings in 1774." See Merrill Jensen, ed., English Historical Documents' American Colonial Documents to 1776 (New York, 1955), 802.

[66] Galloway, Candid Examination, 10-11.

[67] Ibid., 14-15.

[68] Ibid., 27.

69 Ibid., 16, 60. Galloway wrote that under his Plan, "no law can be binding on America, to which the people, by their representatives, have not previously given their consent; this is the essence of liberty...." ibid., 68-69.

BIBLIOGRAPHY

A list of books cited.

Primary Sources:

Adams, Charles Francis, ed., The Works of John Adams, 10 vols. (Boston, 1856).

Allen, James, "Diary of James Allen, Esq., of Philadelphia, Counsellor-at-law, 1770-1778," Pennsylvania Magazine, IX (1885), 176-196, 278-296, 424-441.

Bailyn, Bernard, Pamphlets of the American Revolution, 1750-1776 (Cambridge, 1965).

Blackstone, Sir William, Commentaries of the Laws of England, 4 vols. (New York, 1856).

Bolingbroke, Henry St. John, Works, 4 vols. (Phil., 1841).

Burke, Edmund, Works, 4 vols. (Boston, 1839).

Burlamaqui, J. J., The Principles of Natural and Political Law, trans. Thomas Nugent, 2 vols. (London, 1784).

Butterfield, L. H., ed., Diary and Autobiography of John Adams, 4 vols. (New York, 1964).

------------, The Earliest Diary of John Adams, June 1753-April 1756, Sept. 1758 - January 1759 (Cambridge, 1966).

Chinard, Gilbert, The Commonplace Book of Thomas Jefferson: A Reportory of His Ideas on Government (Baltimore, 1926).

Coke, Sir Edward, The Institutes of the Laws of England, 4 vols. (London, 1747).

-------------, _Reports_, 6 vols. (London, 1826).

Colbourn, Trevor, "A Pennsylvania Farmer at the Court of King George, John Dickinson's London Letters, 1754 - 1756," _Pennsylvania Magazine of History and Biography_, LXXXVI (1962), 241-286, 417-452.

Dexter, Franklin B., ed., _A Selection from the Correspondence... of Jared Ingersoll_ (New Haven Colonial Society, 1918).

Dexter, George, ed., "Record Book of the Suffolk Bar,1770 - 1805," Massachusetts Historical Society _Proceedings._ XIX (1881-82), 141-179.

Dickinson, John, Essay on the Constitutional Power of Great Britain over the Colonies in America, 1774," _Pennsylvania Archives_, 2d Ser., III, 565-622.

-------------, _The Late Regulations Respecting the British Colonies on the Continent of America Considered, in A Letter from A Gentlemen in Philadelphia to his Friend in London_ (Philadelphia, 1765).

-------------, _To My Opponents In the Late Elections of Councillor for the County of Philadelphia, and of President of the Supreme Executive Council of Pennsylvaniania, 1783_ (Library of Congress).

-------------, _Writing of John Dickinson_, ed., Paul Leicester Ford (Philadelphia, 1895).

Foulke, Samuel, "Fragments of a Journal Kept by Samuel Foulke, of Bucks County, while a Member of the Colonial Assembly of

Pennsylvania, 1762-4," Pennsylvania Magazine, V (1881), 60-73.

----------, The Pennsylvania Assembly in 1761-2. A Memorandum Kept by Samuel Foulke," Pennsylvania Magazine, VIII (1884), 407-13.

Franklin, Benjamin, Autobiography, ed. Leonard W. Labaree (New Haven and London, 1964).

----------------, The Papers of Benjamin Franklin, ed. by Leonard W. Labaree, 13 vols. (New Haven, 1959).

Galloway, Joseph, Advertisement to the Publick (Philadelphia, 1765).

--------------, Americanus Examined, and his Principles Compared with Those of the Approved Advocates for America, by A Pennsylvanian (Philadelphia, 1774).

--------------, Arguments on Both Sides in the Dispute between Great Britain and her Colonies, 1774," New Jersey Archives. 1st Ser., X, 478-93.

------------, A Candid Examination of the Mutual Claims of Great Britain and the Colonies, With A Plan of Accommodation on Constitutional Principles (New York, 1775).

-------------, Historical and Political Reflections On The Rise and Progress of the American Rebellion (London, 1780).

-------------, Political Reflections on the Late Colonial Governments: In which their Original Constitutional Defects are Pointed Out, and Shown to have Naturally Produced the

Rebellion, which has Unfortunately Terminated in the Dismemberment of the British Empire (London, 1783).

-------------, The Speech in Answer to the Speech of John Dickinson (Philadelphia, 1764).

----------, A True and Impartial State of the Province of Pennsylvania (Philadelphia, 1759).

Goebel, Julius, Jr., ed., The Law Practice of Alexander Hamilton, Documents and Commentary (New York, 1964).

Hale, Sir Matthew, "Preface," in Henry Rolle, Unabridgement des Plusiers Cases et Resolutions del Common Ley (London, 1668).

Hazard, Samuel, Annals of Pennsylvania...1609-1682 (Philadelphia, 1850).

Howell, T. B., A Complete Collection of State Trials 21 vols. (London, 1816).

Hume, David, The History of England from the Invasion of Julius Caesar to the Abduction of James the Second 1688 6 vols. (New York, 1859).

Inderwick, F. A., ed., A Calendar of the Inner Temple Records, 3 vols. (London, 1901).

Jacobson, David L., ed., The English Libertarian Heritage, John Trenchard and Thomas Gordon in the Independent Whig and Cato's Letters (New York, 1965).

Jefferson, Thomas, The Papers of Thomas Jefferson. ed. by Julian Boyd, 17 vols. (Princeton, 1950).

Jensen, Merrill, ed., English Historical Documents: American Colonial Documents to 1776 (New York, 1955).

Machiavelli, Niccolo, Discourses on the First Decade of Titus Livius (London, 1883).

Molesworth, Robert, An Account of Denmark as it was in the Year 1692 (London, 1738).

Montesquieu, Charles de Secondat, Baron de, The Spirit of the Laws, trans. by Thomas Nugent, 2 vols. (London, 1773).

Morgan, Edmund S., ed., Prologue to Revolution: Sources and Documents on the Stamp Act Crisis, 1764-1766 (Chapel Hill, 1959).

Rapin-Thomas, Paul, The History of England, trans. by N. Tindal (London, 1723).

Sowerby, E. Millicent, Catalogue of the Library of Thomas Jefferson, 5 vols. (Library of Congress, 1952).

Syrett, Harold C., and Jacob E. Cooke, eds., The Papers of Alexander Hamilton (New York, 1961).

Walker, Lewis Burd, ed., Extracts from the Letterbook of Chief Justice William Allen (n.p., 1897).

Wilson, James, The Works of James Wilson, ed. by Robert Green McCloskey, 2 vols. (Cambridge, 1967).

Wroth, L. Kinvin, and Hiller B. Zobel, eds., Legal Papers of John Adams. 3 vols. (New York, 1968).

Periodicals:

Dunham, William H., Jr., "Doctrines of Allegiance in Late Medieval English Law," New York University Law Review, XXVI (1951), 41-75.

Eaton, Clement, "Mirror of a Southern Colonial Lawyer: The Fee Books of Patrick Henry, Thomas Jefferson, and Waightsill Avery," William and Mary Quarterly. 3d ser., VIII (1951), 520-34.

Goebel, Julius, "King's Law and Local Custom in Seventeenth Century New England," Columbia Law Review, XXXI (1931), 416-48.

Haskett, Richard C., "William Paterson, Attorney General of New Jersey Public Office and Private Profit in the American Revolution, "William and Mary Quarterly, 3d. ser., VII (1950), 26-38.

Haskins, George L., "A Problem in the Reception of the Common Law in the Colonial Period," University of Pennsylvania Law Review (1949), 842-53.

Hutson, James H.,"Benjamin Franklin and Pennsylvania Politics, 1751-1755: A Reappraisal," A Pennsylvania Magazine of History and Biography, XCIII (1969), 303-71.

Katz, Stanley M., "Looking Backward, The Early History of American Law," University of Chicago Law Review, XXXIII

(1966), 867-84.

Leonard, Sister Joan de Lourdes, C.S.J., "Elections in Colonial Pennsylvania," William and Mary Quarterly, 3d. Ser., XI (1954), 385-401.

Meehan, Thomas R., Courts, Cases, and Counselors in Revolutionary Pennsylvania," Pennsylvania Magazine of History and Biography, XLI (1967), 3-34.

Morris, Richard B., "Legalism versus Revolutionary Doctrine In New England," New England Quarterly (1931), 195-215.

Nash, Gary B., "The Framing of Government in Pennsylvania, Ideas in Contact with Reality," William and Mary Quarterly, 3d. Ser., XXIII (1966), 183-209.

Savelle, Max, Nationalism and Other Loyalties in the American Revolution,"American Historical Review,LXVII(1962)),901-23.

Secondary:

Adams, George Burton, The Origin of the English Constitution (New Haven, 1912).

Adams, Randolph G., Political Ideas of the American Revolution: Britannic-American Contribution to the Problem of Imperial Organization 1765 to 1775 (North Carolina, 1922).

Bailyn, Bernard, The Ideological Origins of the American Revolution (Cambridge, 1967).

Baldwin, Ernest H., Joseph Galloway, Loyalist Politician (Philadelphia, 1902).

Boorstin, Daniel, The Americans: The Colonial Experience (New

York, 1964).

Boyd, Julian, Anglo-American Union: John Galloway's Plans to Preserve the British Empire. 1774-1778 (Philadelphia, 1941).

Chinard, Gilbert, Thomas Jefferson, The Apostle of Americanism (Boston, 1929).

Colbourn, Trevor, The Lamp of Experience, Whig History and the Intellectual Origins of the American Revolution (Chapel Hill, 1965).

Dillon, Dorothy Rita, The New York Triumvirate, A Study of the Legal and Political Careers of William Livingston, John Morin Scott, William Smith. Jr. (New York, 1949).

Gipson, Lawrence Henry, The British Empire Before the American Revolution, 13 vols. (New York, 1960).

Hamlin, Paul M., Legal Education in Colonial New York (New York, 1939).

------------ and Charles E Baker, Supreme Court of Judicature of the Province of New York. 1691-1704, 3 vols. (New York Historical Society, 1952).

Harvey, Ray Forrest, Jean Jacques Burlamaqui: A Liberal Tradition in American Constitutionalism (Chapel Hill, 1937).

Haskins, George Lee, Law and Authority in Early Massachusetts, A Study in Tradition and Design (New York, 1960).

Holdsworth, Sir William, A History of English Law, 12 vols. (London, 1938).

Jacobson, David L., John Dickinson and Joseph Galloway,1764 -

1764 - 1776: A Study in Contrasts (unpubl. Ph.D. diss., Princeton University, 1959).

Kliger, Samuel, _The Goths in England, A Study in Seventeenth and Eighteenth Century Thought_ (Cambridge, 1952).

Knollenberg, Bernhard, _Origin of the American Revolution: 1759-1766_ (New York, 1960).

Labaree, Leonard W., _Royal Government in America, Study of the British Colonial System before 1783_ (New Haven, 1930).

Land, Aubrey C., _The Dulanys of Maryland, A Biographical Study of Daniel Dulany, the Elder (1685-1753) and Daniel Dulany, the Younger (1722-1797)_ (Baltimore, 1955).

Loftie, W. J., _The Inns of Court and Chancery_ (London, 1895).

McIlwain, Charles Howard, _The American Revolution Constitutional Interpretation_ (Ithaca, 1923).

Main, Jackson Turner, _The Social Structure of Revolutionary America_ (Princeton, 1965).

Maitland, Frederick W., _The Constitutional History of England_ (Cambridge, 1955).

Malone, Dumas, _Jefferson the Virginian_ (Boston, 1948).

Mark, Irving, _Agrarian Conflicts in Colonial New York_, _1711-1775_ (New York, 1940).

Meade, Robert Donthat, _Patrick Henry. Patriot in the Making_ (Philadelphia and New York, 1957).

Monaghan, Frank, _John Jay: Defender of Liberty Against Kings and Peoples_ (New York, 1935).

Morgan, Edmund S. and Helen M., The Stamp Act Crisis: Prologue to Revolution (New York, 1963).

Parrington, Vernon L., The Colonial Mind, 1620-1800 (New York, 1927).

Pearce, Robert R., A Guide to the Inns of Court and Chancery (London, 1855).

Pocock, J. G. A., The Ancient Constitution and the Feudal Law: A Study of English Historical Thought in the Seventeenth Century (Cambridge, 1957).

Pole, J. R., Political Representation in England and the Origins of the American Republic (New York, 1966).

Pound, Roscoe, The Lawyer from Antiquity to Modern Times: With Particular Reference to the Development of Bar Associations in the United States (Minnesota, 1953).

Powell, John H., John Dickinson, Penman of the Revolution (unpubl. Ph.D. diss., University of Iowa, 1938).

Robbins, Caroline, The Eighteenth-Century Commonwealthman: Studies in the Transmission, Development and Circumstance of English Liberal Thought from the Restoration of Charles II until the war with the thirteen Colonies (Cambridge, 1961).

Schuyler, Robert Livingston, Parliament and the British Empire, Some Constitutional Controversies Concerning Imperial Legislative Jurisdiction (New York, 1929).

Selsam, J. Paul, Pennsylvania Constitution of 1776: A Study in Revolutionary Democracy (Philadelphia, 1936).

Shipton, Clifford K., Sibley's Harvard Graduates. Biographical Sketches of those who Attended Harvard, 15 vols. (Boston, 1960).

Smith, Charles Page, James Wilson, Founding Father (Chapel Hill, 1956).

Smith, H. F. Russell, Harrington and his Oceana, A Study of A Seventeenth Century Utopia and its Influence in America (Cambridge, 1914).

Stille, Charles, Life and Times of John Dickinson, 1732-1802 (Philadelphia, 1819).

Tolles, Frederick B., Meeting House and Counting House, The Quaker Merchants of Colonial Philadelphia 1682-1783 (New York, 1963).

Waters, John, Jr., Otis Family in Provincial and Revolutionary Massachusetts (Chapel Hill, 1968).

Werner, Raymond Clarence, Joseph Galloway, His Life and Times (unpubl. Ph.D. diss., University of Iowa, 1927).